BISCUIT JOINER:

A Woodworker's How-To Guide To Biscuit Joinery

With Four Project Plans

2017 Revised Edition

A How-To Workbook From Positive Imaging, LLC

A. William Benitez

BISCUIT JOINER:

A Woodworker's How-To Guide To Biscuit Joinery

Reintroducing My Favorite Joinery Tool With Four Project Plans

2017 Revised Edition

By A. William Benitez

Published By
Positive Imaging, LLC
9016 Palace Parkway
Austin, TX 78748 USA

Cover, photographs, and drawings by A. William Benitez

ISBN 9780985687625

ABOUT THE COVER

I used a photo of the dining room set in my home for the cover because every aspect of the set involved the use of biscuit joinery. I built this set in a small shop after retiring from woodworking after more than thirty years. I'm now a writer and publisher and since I'm not retired and still build woodworking projects, retirement is probably not be an accurate term.

Because I was working on other things, it took many months to get this entire project built. When I did work on the set, the joinery was straight forward involving standard joints so it didn't delay the work.

The delays were caused by the lack of time and the hand carving of many surfaces, especially the entire table top. The carving was done entirely by hand with a British 1/16 inch cove, 1 inch wide gouge used without a hammer or mallet.

The tabletop was made of 8/4 (2 inch) thick solid maple which I purchased rough and planed down to 1 3/ 4 inch thick and then glued up and cut to shape. I used biscuits in the joints for gluing up the table solely to maintain the alignment of the boards and, once clamped, I took care to make certain all the boards were even with one another and all the glue ooze was wiped clean to limit my sanding. Once the table was completely sanded, the endless hours of hand carving began.

The legs on the table were designed to be different from most tables. Instead of being on the outside corners of the table or forming a trestle, they form a cross pattern and are centered of each side of the table. They were assembled using three biscuits in each joint for extra strength and then rounded over and a hand carved feature added to each leg.

The chairs also have many features but those are discussed in the project photo section of the book so I won't describe here.

The doors on the china cabinet are also interesting but I have a close up of them in the project photo section of the book where I describe them in detail.

ABOUT THE BOOK AND THE METHODS

I wrote this book because I sincerely believe the Biscuit Joiner is a great joinery tool to help woodworkers do quality work without all the time and skill involved in using traditional joinery methods. While I believe this book could be helpful to woodworkers making a living with their skills, it is aimed at the large number of woodworkers across the world who work with wood because they just love woodworking.

Many of those woodworkers believe in traditional joinery and will continue to use it and I would never consider discouraging that because it is challenging, produces beautiful work, and provides a great learning experience. However, there are options and this book presents one of those options to any interested woodworker.

To make biscuit joinery as easy to understand as possible I have included four simple yet useful project plans of pieces whose construction is based strongly on the Biscuit Joiner and can be completed in a weekend. For some it may take longer but the important thing is to realize the value of the Biscuit Joiner in creating such projects

Also included are photographs of projects I built using the Biscuit Joiner. Even though I built hundreds of large and complex projects for customers over the years of owning and operating my woodworking business, I have limited the photos to projects I built for our home over the past few years in the small home shop I have since leaving the woodworking business. I hope these motivate readers to build similar projects for their own home or even for customers.

Finally, I want to emphasize the importance of taking advantage of your own creative abilities when working with the simple project plans in the book or with any project you decide to build. While project plans can be helpful, I have never taken them as carved in granite. They are basically clear ideas of how a certain project can be built but definitely not the only way. Feel free to use the project plans exactly as designed but please don't hesitate to change them, improve them, make them your own.

I have answers that work for me now and have worked for me for years but they are not the only answers nor even the best answers. They are just my answers and chances are quite good that your ideas and answers will be better. I encourage you to explore them fully.

To further encourage you to make changes to the projects, this book was designed with lots of white space at the margins, between the paragraphs and it even has pages throughout for your notes and calculations.

Explore the possibilities of the four projects with complete instructions and drawings but also check out the projects that I built for my home and take the ideas from any you like and redesign them to fit your needs. Feel free to make the ideas your own. I look forward to hearing about your projects. Contact me at bill@positive-imaging.com.

CONTENTS

Notes

PREFACE

I've worked on variations of this book over the past dozen years. The idea for it began about twenty years ago while I was still operating my woodworking shop in Austin, Texas. A representative of the Skil Power Tool company contacted me about performing power tool demonstrations at the Austin and San Antonio, Texas Home Depot stores. Even though my business was doing fairly well, the demonstrations would take place only on weekends and seemed like an interesting way to make some extra money for my business. It also occurred to me that I might run into some potential customers for cabinets and furniture projects.

The Power Tool Demonstrations

The Skil Power Tool company furnished all the tools since none of my shop tools were made by Skil. The job was simple enough. The Skil representative made the arrangements with the Store and I would arrive early Saturday morning and set up a small, usually about 4 foot by 8 foot, shop area for the tools and benches Skil provided. Then I would design a small, simple project and select the lumber for it from the Home Depot stock, usually it was simply 3/4 inch thick white pine.

Using the Skil tools I would build the project in the small shop area and answer questions about the tools, how best to use them, and how to build the projects. I would usually do this from about 8 a.m. to 4 p.m. with a short lunch break.

The Tools and The Shop Space

Obviously, this was a marketing effort to encourage the store customers to buy the Skil power tools but the goal of the demonstrations was to show more than the capability of the tools. They also served to show that nice projects could be built in a small space using inexpensive tools. There was a nice collection of power tools including a table saw, circular saw, jig saw, router, belt sander, drill, finish sander, and most importantly to me, a Biscuit Joiner. The unique advantages of the Biscuit Joiner facilitated the quick assembly and glue up of projects so there was always a completed project at the end of each demonstration. The successfully completed projects generated many questions and power tool sales for the store.

The Projects

There were many projects during the year or so that I performed the demonstrations but the four detailed in this book were the most popular. For that reason I refined the instructions and the drawings for them and would sometimes hand out copies at the demonstrations. The projects include the bookcase, the range shelf, the table, and the most popular by far, the chair. The projects were small because of the limited space available to build them and the table and chair were geared especially for parents to build for their kids. I made dozens of them for friends and family and still do once in a while in my small shop.

The small bookcase, which was well suited to paperbacks and VHS tapes when they were popular, can easily be altered to accommodate CDs and DVDs but was never as popular as the other projects. The range shelf was popular with adults who wanted them to put on their range. During the time I was making them someone dubbed it "Home on the Range" which I thought was appropriate. I still get an occasional request for this project.

When I built the projects during the demonstrations I always used the inexpensive white pine that is so readily available at Home Depot stores. However, the projects can easily be made of any lumber and they look quite good in oak or other hardwoods. In addition to using other woods, the basic plans can be adjusted in several ways to personalize it to your own use. I always advise people to use the project plans only as a guide. They are not carved in granite.

The Biscuit Joiner

Obviously, it takes several different tools to build these projects but, as with most wood projects, joinery is of significant importance as it affects the strength, longevity, and the appearance of such projects. For that reason my emphasis is on the Biscuit Joiner as the main tool for building the projects.

By the time I started these demonstrations I had been using Biscuit Joiners for years and felt most people were aware of their existence. It turned out that few people had any concept of the Biscuit Joiner and its many uses. Once they realized the potential, many of those viewing the demonstrations purchased Biscuit Joiners and dropped by for tips on more ways to use them. Since it is one of my favorite tools, that was an enjoyable part of the demonstrations.

Putting It All Together

As the tools, small shop space, projects, and the Biscuit Joiner all came together I realized that it would be a good topic for a small helpful book. My first effort was just a small booklet with a little information about the projects that I gave away to peak interest in a woodworking business book I wrote at the time. Occasionally I would add something to it but it remained just a booklet for a long time.

After completing my latest book on the woodworking business I was spending a lot of time looking at woodworking related books and reading comments and reviews about them. There were a few books about the Biscuit Joiner but most of the reviews indicated they lacked the kind of information that might be useful to woodworkers, novice or pro, who wanted to use them as a joinery tool. I decided that using those old project plans and instructions together with more updated information and photos of projects built using the Biscuit Joiner might serve as a valuable guide for woodworkers.

This book is the outcome of old and new information about using my favorite woodworking tool, the Biscuit Joiner. I hope you find it useful and I welcome your questions or comments at bill@positive-imaging.com

Avoiding Controversy

There actually is some controversy regarding Biscuit Joiners. It usually stems from power tool users who either believe Biscuit Joiners are not efficient and accurate power tools, or others who feel other joinery methods are better than biscuit joinery.

This especially comes up with those who use dowels and for some reason seem to consider the use of the Biscuit Joiner an affront. I wrote this book because, based on years of first-hand experience, I believe the Biscuit Joiner to be a valuable tool for wood joinery. I know it isn't the only tool for this purpose nor is it the only joinery method. It's simply one that I like and want to share with other woodworkers.

While this book may be of value to some professional woodworkers, it was written to help home woodworkers to build projects better and faster by taking advantage of the capabilities of Biscuit Joiners. Whether you use the information and make use of biscuit joinery is entirely up to you. After all my years of experience I know what Biscuit Joiners are capable of and how to use them efficiently and effectively. I hope you will find that experience, as shared in this book, of real value. I also know there are many ways to build woodworking projects and woodworkers have their own methods. It is not my intent to prove that using Biscuit Joiners is better than any of those other methods nor do I intend to argue with anyone about this. Each woodworker should evaluate the information available and make their own decision.

INTRODUCTION

I've always found woodworking interesting, challenging, and enjoyable but doing it as a full-time professional is entirely different and each woodworker handles the tasks involved in running a successful business differently. When I started my woodworking business I was running my writing and consulting service but my business dried up because of federal funding cuts. Doesn't sound much different from what many people are suffering as I write this book. Fortunately, I was raised in construction with my contractor dad and had extensive woodworking skills already.

Starting From Scratch

Starting a new business when you just lost another one is not easy and it's critical to get the cash flow going quickly. You are not just growing a business, you have to make a living at the same time. I didn't have the luxury of speculating and building projects to sell at some store or some corner location. I needed jobs that paid promptly and that meant getting contracted work for which I collected a deposit and got paid in full immediately upon completion.

Developing A Plan

My plan was to design and build specialty cabinets and furniture not readily available in stores. While I was willing to build kitchen cabinets, I knew that it would be difficult to compete with those companies who specialized in kitchen cabinets and had space for large kitchen jobs.

Having a plan is important but when you really need regular cash flow and are just getting started, flexibility is critical. To keep the money flowing I was open to all kinds of jobs until I developed a clientele for the kinds of cabinets and furniture I wanted to build. Those extra jobs included a variety of home repairs, some carpentry jobs, and even building a coffin for a dog.

It took time but the work I wanted to do started to come in regularly and people called me to design and build their cabinets or furniture and then referred me to others. As I began to do those jobs it was clear that increasing profit was essential to continued success. Part of that could be handled by increasing my prices as my popularity increased but there was a limit to that. Another option was to take less time to do the work and here is where the Biscuit Joiner came in.

Good joinery without nails and screws takes time and with the Biscuit Joiner I found it was possible to develop methods to help me deliver products to please my customers in less time while still charging the same prices. I called these methods simplified woodworking.

For over thirty years I designed quality cabinets and furniture that pleased my customers and built them much quicker using these simplified methods and more specifically using the Biscuit Joiner to create the joinery for assembly.

Simplified Woodworking

Simplified woodworking just refers to simpler, easier and faster methods than what some would consider traditional woodworking methods. It's important to emphasize this is in no way a put down of traditional methods or tools. Even among traditional woodworkers there are different ways to do things. Simplified woodworking is simply an alternative method some woodworkers may find useful. The main goal of these simplified methods is to facilitate the quick completion of woodworking projects thereby facilitating a reasonable price for the product and a fair profit for the woodworker.

It's difficult to clearly define simplified woodworking because it can vary depending on the project so instead I'll cover how these methods evolved and some of the basic techniques. As I said previously, when I started my woodworking business it seemed evident it would be difficult for me to make a good living with my customer base using traditional woodworking methods. There were some woodworkers doing it, but very few. Well known woodworkers, who charged high prices for their work usually, supplemented their income by writing books and articles about their work based on a degree of fame. I was far from famous and needed to make a living with my woodworking.

Quality and Profit

Realizing the importance of both quality and profit, I needed ways to complete my work faster and at a lower cost while still maintaining a high degree of quality and making a reasonable profit. I began compiling ideas to make things simpler and therefore faster. One of the major questions I faced was "What kind of joinery can I use on my furniture jobs?" This was an important question because mortise and tenon, dovetails, finger joints, dados, etc., while definitely effective can be time consuming. Dowels were not the answer because I didn't believe they were strong enough because of inadequate glue surface and I found them more difficult to align.

Nails and screws provided a good alternative for some cabinets such as those in kitchens. Screw holes could be plugged and nail holes could be filled. The combination of nails for assembly and screws for strength worked quite well for many kitchens but it was definitely not the best answer for pieces of furniture. Although with shop made plugs it did give an acceptable appearance.

A Simpler Joinery Method

I concluded that for me to build furniture projects economically would require a simpler joinery method. Butt joints are certainly simple and fast but have little strength. My answer was to use the Biscuit Joiner or plate joiner to reinforce all joints. This one tool helped me build many beautiful projects quickly and easily without complex joinery or holes to plug or fill. Sharing the many ways the Biscuit Joiner served me then and still does is a major reason for this book

To help you better understand how best to use the Biscuit Joiner, I have included complete project plans for four small projects that can be constructed easily using the Biscuit Joiner. These projects are intended to show various ways to use a Biscuit Joiner to build projects. They are not complex and, with the clear instructions and drawings included, can probably be built easily by most novice woodworkers.

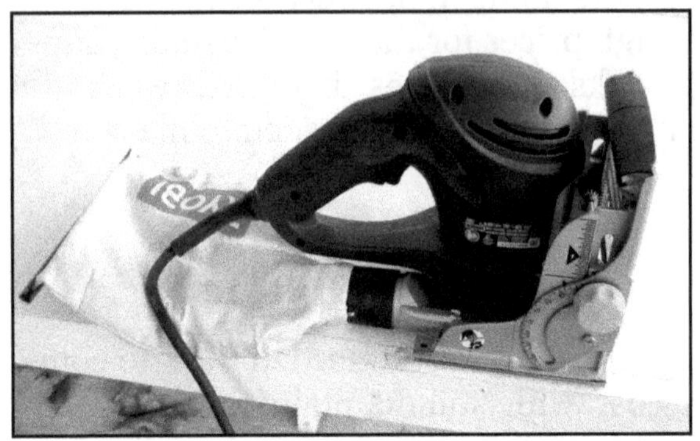

Besides the four project plans there are photos of more than a dozen projects that I built for my home using biscuit joinery. There is also a section of the various wood joints possible with the Biscuit Joiner and a full section with clear photos showing ways to use the Biscuit Joiner.

Also included are some final notes that should be of great help to anyone making use of the Biscuit Joiner and a Glossary of woodworking terms.

1

THE BISCUIT JOINER

The job of a cabinetmaker/woodworker varies in different parts of the country. In Florida, during the 80s when I was starting my woodworking business, it involved heavy use of plastic laminate, not just for countertops but also for cabinet surfaces. Having an account at a wholesale laminate distributor was essential. It was at one of those distributors where I ran into my first Biscuit Joiner. It was on display with other power tools and at first sight I recognized it's potential as a joinery tool and knew it could save me hours of work and contribute to the quality of all my cabinet and furniture jobs.

My First Biscuit Joiner

The Biscuit Joiner brand was Virutex and it was made in Spain. At $335.00 it was a lot of money for me at the time. Nevertheless, I bought it immediately because it was clearly the joinery breakthrough I had been looking for. Like most Biscuit Joiners, the instructions with it were inadequate but sufficient to get me started and in short order I was a Biscuit Jointer expert using it to save time and deliver quality cabinets and furniture.

Since I had never seen a Biscuit Joiner before I didn't know if other companies made them. I now know there were other brands available, especially the commercial model Lamello. Now many other power tool companies have added Biscuit Joiners to their tool lines and the prices begin as low at $80.00. At first some companies even developed conversion kits to attach to grinders or routers to make Biscuit Joiners but I've always felt it was better to buy a tool that was originally designed as a Biscuit Joiner.

My emphasis on the Biscuit Joiner is not meant to diminish the value of all the tools you would normally use in woodworking. They play a role in simplified woodworking but the Biscuit Joiner is the single most important tool for joinery because it allows you to create strong and easily aligned joints on almost any cabinet or furniture project. Most importantly for a professional woodworker, it saves time without affecting quality so it can contribute to profit if projects are priced correctly.

Learning To Use It Carefully

Learning to use a biscuit joiner is not difficult but getting good results does require careful handling. Biscuit joiners cut a matching slot on two separate surfaces. Then the two surfaces are joined together by placing a compressed wood biscuit or wafer with glue into the matching slots. Because it can make the work go faster, some Biscuit Joiner users tend to rush and carelessly align the tool with the work. This can create joints that are sloppy, weak and often unattractive.

Because the biscuits (wafers) are made of compressed beech, they begin swelling immediately upon contact with the wet glue. This facilitates short clamping times. The momentary looseness of the biscuit as the glue dries allows for minor adjustment of the two parts during clamping to make certain the parts are perfectly aligned.

Unlike with dowels, minor adjustments are possible before the glue sets. It is a short open time but it does provide a unique advantage. Naturally, you can't make up for major sloppiness with these adjustments because it is only about 1/32 inch but it can be very helpful during assembly of projects.

As soon as the glue dries you have a strong joint. The biscuits provide a great deal more strength than dowels because they have at least twenty times the glue surface but, more importantly, all the glue surface is on the long grain of the wood. Because of the round shape of the dowels, much of the glue surface faces the end grain of the wood which doesn't glue well. Obviously, using the biscuit joiner carefully is important if the two slots are to align properly. As with any woodworking tool, careless handling will lead to poor results.

Biscuit joinery can be used in many ways. It can be used in lieu of mortise and tenon joinery to assemble tables, chairs and other pieces. However, it is important to remember that even though biscuit joinery is stronger than dowels, it is not stronger than mortise and tenon joinery.

Business Note: If a customer requests and expects mortise and tenon joinery and you only use biscuit joinery, this should be explained to your customer before accepting the job because they are not the same thing.

Biscuit joinery can also be used in lieu of dados when building bookcases. Biscuit joinery works well to assemble frames of any kind including cabinet doors and face frames. It is very useful for applying solid wood edging to an infinite number of plywood projects.

While operating my shop in Florida I found another unique advantage when building cabinets covered with plastic laminate. Since it is wise to laminate the inside of cabinet parts that require laminate before assembly, with the Biscuit Joiner you could cover all the inside surfaces with laminate and then cut the biscuit slots through the laminate so that you would still have a good glue surface available to hold the cabinet together. I used this technique on many cabinets over the years.

Notes

2

CHOOSING A BISCUIT JOINER

If you don't already own a biscuit joiner, choosing one is the first step. There are many brands to choose from even though the popularity of biscuit joiners seems to have waned. Recently I read a comment from a woodworker indicating his feeling that biscuit joiners were inherently inaccurate. In truth, the same could be said about most power tools. Carelessly used, table saws, circular saws, routers, sanders, and others could be considered inherently inaccurate.

Controlling Power Tools

Years ago, when I performed the power tool demonstrations at Home Depot stores for Skil, one of the most popular power tools with many of the store's customers was the table scroll saw which I demonstrated by cutting out names for individuals. People loved seeing their name cut out and some immediately purchased a scroll saw. Many of the purchasers would bring their scroll saws back the next weekend complaining it wouldn't cut straight and failed to make a name when they attempted one. Each time I would hook up the saw, ask them what name they wanted to cut, and immediately cut it out without difficulty.

These customers were convinced that the problem was with the tool instead with them. Power tools, whether scroll saws, biscuit joiners, or others must be controlled by the user. The scroll saw can't follow a line on the wood it can only cut the wood, you have to guide it along the line. I helped some who managed to catch on but some just wanted a refund because they were absolutely certain there was something wrong with the machine. Others were convinced the problem was the quality of the inexpensive scroll saw. It's certainly true there is a difference in the degree of precision between an expensive trade tool and a consumer brand tool but, like these scroll saws, both are capable of a good job if handled competently. Choosing a Biscuit Joiner is important but all the available brands will do the job adequately if handled carefully.

Top Of The Line

To me, Lamello is the top of the line in Biscuit Joiners. With prices ranging from about $300.00 to over $700.00 they are the choice of many professional woodworkers. Even though these are precision tools, for the person working in a home shop there is no need for this large investment. Even a full-time professional woodworker can function adequately with a much less costly Biscuit Joiner.

Which one should you buy? Over the years I have used the Virutex, Skil, Freud, Craftsman, Porter-Cable, DeWalt and Ryobi biscuit joiners ranging in price from about $100.00 to $335.00. I used the Virutex and the Freud for years and would definitely recommend them but my favorite now is the Ryobi. In spite of its low price it consistently does a good job for me and it has an efficient fence that doesn't require removal. It simply folds up out of the way. Since I work mostly without the fence on my Biscuit Joiner, this is an important feature.

All Worked Well

All of the biscuit joiners I used performed reasonably well. The Virutex was excellent but more expensive than most. The Skil unit was priced fairly low and worked reasonably well but the last time I looked it was only available at eBay. I used this unit every weekend for about a year while performing power tool demonstrations for the Skil Power Tool Company. The one problem I had with the Skil Biscuit Joiner was the dust chute feeding into the dust bag was too narrow and it would clog regularly. It also had a fence that can only be removed and adjusted by using an Allen wrench. I prefer a fence that doesn't require complete removal and will adjust with handles as part of the tool. These fences also resolve the issue of losing the screws to hold the fence in place while it is removed.

Regarding the clogging dust chute, over the years I have found this to be a common problem with biscuit joiners and other tools. On my biscuit joiners I avoid the problem by removing the dust chute completely and making a right angle sawdust exhaust using a pvc elbow I ground down slightly to fit tightly on the Biscuit Joiner. This guides the saw dust away from me when making a cut and avoids the problem of the clogged chute and having to regularly empty the too small dust bags.

Low Priced Models

If you want something new and are on a tight budget, Sears has a fairly good unit. One look and it’s obvious that Ryobi is making the Craftsman Biscuit Joiners. This is no detriment since Ryobi makes a good unit. These units are a real bargain at under $100. It's a good tool for the home workshop and it will do everything like the more expensive models. Since it is made by Ryobi it has the same great fence that allows you to set from 45 degrees through 90 degrees all the way to 135 degrees. For certain jobs this feature is very handy. The Ryobi also retails for around $100 at home improvement stores.

The Freud biscuit joiner is an excellent tool that I used for many years. It is a little more expensive than the Skil but it is a more precise tool and the biscuit joiner assembly is made of metal. For a long time this was my only biscuit joiner and it performed well. So if you can find a good deal on one don't hesitate. These have been around for a while and you may be able to find a good used one.

Higher Priced Different Designs

For those with a larger budget there are other options. Porter Cable made a totally different biscuit joiner that some people swore by. The design was unique and like all Porter Cable tools, it worked well. The price was higher than many of the other units but well worth it for the quality. The one shortcoming of this unit was the fence had to be removed with an Allen wrench inviting the possibility of lost parts. I didn’t care for the feel of the handle but that was just personal preference and not a reflection on the unit. The newest Porter Cable is another design that looks better but I have never used one. Since Porter Cable makes good products it would be worth checking out.

Another Biscuit Joiner in the $250 or so price range is the DeWalt. It has a very good fence assembly and comes with the DeWalt quality reputation. On this one I didn't care for the placement of the switch but again that's a personal preference and should not reflect on this machine. This outlines some of the many choices. If you want to do good work faster, buy one of these machines. Once you use one you will wonder how you ever got along without it.

3

USING THE BISCUIT JOINER

Your new Biscuit Joiner will probably include a small book of basic instructions to help get you started. Some of these contain fairly good but limited information. Unfortunately some users won't take the time to read even a small book before starting to use the tool. Since the Biscuit Joiner is basically a small saw facilitating controlled joinery cuts, it requires careful and practiced handling to get precision results. In addition to making the work go faster, an important objective is to create quality projects and that is only possible if you know how to make good use of the Biscuit Joiner. The more knowledge you have about how to use the Biscuit Joiner the better, easier, and faster your work will be. The next few paragraphs contain information I have found helpful when using biscuit joiners.

Test Cuts

This first tip is one few people have the patience for but it will save you time and frustration. Make a test cut every time you change the settings on your biscuit joiner. When you change the size of the biscuit, check for correct depth. The correct depth is slightly more than one half the overall depth of the biscuit. Place the biscuit in your test cut and make a pencil mark across the biscuit at the edge of the board with a sharp pencil. Pull out the biscuit and notice the relationship of the line to the center of the biscuit. The pencil mark should be slightly past the center of the biscuit, but only slightly. Don't make the slots too deep. Check the location relative to the edge of the material or the center of the board. If the depth and location are correct you can proceed to cut the slots in the actual work. This does consume time but not as much time as making your cuts incorrectly and winding up with a flawed assembly. This one step will save you many mistakes.

Base and Fence Alignment

Since the accuracy of the biscuit slots is critical to successful biscuit joinery, always make certain the face of the biscuit joiner and the face of the fence are tight and flat against the surfaces of the material to be cut. This is best done by clamping the work piece and controlling the Biscuit Joiner with both hands. This helps you line up the cut and maintain a steady position keeping the Biscuit Joiner from shifting during the cut. Start the biscuit joiner and make certain the torque of the motor has not caused the Biscuit Joiner to move before making the cut. Movement during the cut can cause the blade to enlarge portions of the slot causing poor fit of the wafers. Even if the slots do not enlarge, movement can impede accurate alignment and cause problems during assembly.

When making projects such as bookcases, use the shelves as a straight edge to make your biscuit cuts. For example, place the shelf face down on the line identifying its location. Clamp it in place so it is square and even with the edge of the bookcase sides. Then mark your biscuit locations on the shelf. This one mark will be used for both cuts. When cutting the sides, line the marks with the centerline on the bottom of the biscuit joiner. Hold the biscuit joiner steady keeping the base of the biscuit joiner flat against the edge of the shelf and the fence flat against the side while making the cut. When cutting the shelf edges, line the marks with the centerline on the front of the biscuit joiner. Hold the biscuit joiner steady with the fence tightly against the edge of the shelf and the base tightly against the side. Always make the cuts on the sides before the edge cuts on the shelves. This will ensure that the face cuts are completed accurately even if the clamped piece moves under the pressure of the edge cuts. The few extra moments taken to maintain a steady hold on the biscuit joiner will make the assembly easier and more accurate.

Proper Gluing

It's easy to make a glue mess when assembling a project with biscuits. Proper gluing involves planning each step of the assembly in advance. The most common problem for beginners is using too much glue. Many woodworkers believe the glue has to ooze out everywhere for a strong joint to result. All you need is enough glue in the joint, not all over everything. Applying glue is the same wherever you do it. Not only does too much glue cause a big mess, it's difficult to clean and wasteful. Cleaning up excessive glue is no fun and often leads to a lot of sanding. Biscuits fit tightly and don't require excessive glue for a strong joint.

I suggest purchasing one of the special glue bottles made for biscuit joinery. Some of them are very inexpensive. If you will be using the Biscuit Joiner a lot, purchase a glue container made by Lamello. It is somewhat expensive but has the unique advantage of always dispensing the correct amount of glue into the slot. The other units depend on your skills to determine the amount needed in each joint. After much practice, I can apply the right amount of glue using a standard round glue bottle tip with a small hole. The trick is to apply a thin bead of glue on both sides of the slot just below the surface of the board and straight along the top of the slot. This way the glue will begin to run down both sides of the slot slowly. If the biscuit is inserted promptly, a good bond will result. If you get any ooze out when you put the boards together you should immediately lighten up on the glue for the next joint.

Planning The Glueup

The most important part of planning the glue up of projects with biscuits is to assemble in order to avoid having glue running out of the biscuit slots during the assembly. It really isn't complicated and will save you hours of cleanup, sanding, and frustration. Just consider the obvious fact that glue will run into slots facing up and out of slots facing down. If you put glue into a slot and then turn it to face downward, the glue will promptly begin to run out and make a mess. If you plan your glueup so you will always be putting glue into slots facing up, the mess is avoided. This takes a little planning but it is well worth the effort to avoid a glue mess. Each of the project plans has specific instructions on the best way to cut the biscuit slots and assemble the projects to avoid glue mess.

Notes

4

OTHER TOOLS AND SHOP SPACE

From conversations with woodworkers over the years it's clear that many believe quality woodworking can only be done with higher priced trade or professional grade tools. Commercial grade tools are usually capable of more precision and last longer than consumer grade tools but from personal experience I know quality work is possible with consumer grade tools. Commercial grade tools are better for work requiring extreme precision but then only in the hands of someone sufficiently competent to perform work at that level of precision.

Unless you are a full time professional or have a generous personal budget I suggest you buy consumer brand tools and then install quality accessories on them. These accessories include good quality carbide tipped blades and bits. Most new power tools now come with carbide blades but they are usually low quality blades. It's best to replace them with higher quality blades that will do a better job and last longer. Routers are also much more effective and efficient when used with carbide-tipped bits.

Power Tools For The Shop

As the main topic of this book, it's obvious I believe the Biscuit Joiner is a critical tool for efficiently building quality woodworking projects in the fastest and easiest way possible but it's definitely not the only one. It is one of many tools you need for a basic shop including a table saw, circular saw, belt sander, finish sander, drill, drill press, jig saw, router, and planer together with hand tools and clamps. A band saw and scroll saw are also handy tools to have.

The random orbit sander is another power tool I find useful for faster woodworking. These sanders work much faster than normal orbital or finishing sanders yet they still do a good job. Their high efficiency at sanding surfaces comes from being a combination of disc sander, removing material rapidly with its high speed circular motion, and an orbital sander that smoothing in every direction. With this dual action the circular motion removes the material and the random orbital motion sands out the circular scratches created by the circular motion. It is a great combination that can significantly reduce your sanding time on any project. There are many different models of random orbit sanders. My favorite, and I have not used them all, is the 5" Bosch. It has tested very well with woodworking magazines and I have used one extensively.

Shop Space

Shop space is another important factor. Some woodworkers believe a large shop space is essential for building wood projects. Such a space is certainly helpful for a professional woodworker. When I left the woodworking business I had 1,400 square feet of shop space and, with a large backlog of work, I made use of every inch.

Such a large space is not essential. I have a good friend who ran a lucrative woodworking business for years working out of his two-car garage before he finally moved into a larger shop space. I started my woodworking business in a twelve by twenty-four foot space and worked there for over a year before moving into a larger space. Sometimes larger projects were difficult to fit in that space but I managed.

For the power tool demonstrations for the Skil Power Tool company at Home Depot stores I built the small projects detailed in this book and others in a 4 foot by 8 foot shop area that I set up in any available space at the particular Home Depot I was visiting at the time. With a little planning you can make the best of the space you have available.

5

FINISHING

Finishing is often taken for granted as many people believe anyone can do it with little or no difficulty. To some extent that's true because many people do their own painting. Unfortunately, some of those jobs don't turn out well, especially when it involves painting or staining and clear coating cabinets or furniture. Doing this kind of finish well takes skill and practice.

Disappointing Finishes

During my many years in the woodworking business I ran into some customers who wanted to save money by doing their own finishing. I always discouraged them and my first thought was to turn down the work. However, when you make your living building furniture and cabinets and cash flow is slow, turning down work is seldom an option. On two different jobs I was sorely disappointed by the end result of the finishing job.

One job involved a houseful of beautiful maple furniture including a dining room set and many other pieces throughout the house. I was quite happy with the completed furniture as was the owner. Unfortunately, when I went back to the home and saw the finished product I was sorely disappointed. The pieces not only looked poorly finished and mottled but it was obvious that none of the pieces had been adequately sanded, if at all, between coats because it was quite rough to the touch. This changed the job from one that I was really proud of to one where I was concerned that when they told others who built the furniture they would not explain they had applied the finish.

On another such job I did a complete kitchen in an excellent grade of maple in preparation for a clear finish and instead the owner painted the entire kitchen in an extremely dark color with the same roughness indicating a failure to do any sanding at all.

Finishing can make the difference between a beautiful project and a poor or mediocre one. There are many steps involved in a good finishing job whether you are going to paint the piece or apply a stain and a clear coat. Either way requires following certain important steps to ensure a smooth and attractive look.

Sanding

On both of the jobs described above many finishing mistakes were made but the most significant was the failure to sand between coats of finish. This applies to both clear coats and paint. Fine sanding before a coat of finish is critical for a good job. The surface where the finish will be applied should be smooth to the touch and fully cleaned of all sanding dust before applying the next coat. Before the final coat, the surface should be smooth as glass. With that kind of preparation the finish will turn out really well.

Clear Finishes That I Like

While painting is certainly an option, I've always liked using clear coats on wood to appreciate the color and grain. With some woods a clear coat alone will look beautiful but for others a stain may improve the appearance. Over the years I have used several different clear finishes and have listed them below.

Deft Clear Wood Finish

Deft Clear Wood Finish is one of my favorites. It is basically a brushing lacquer. One of the problems of brushing on a finish is that it often leaves unattractive brush marks on the finished surfaces. Deft overcomes this because it is a self-leveling product that is relatively easy to use. If you follow the instructions on the can carefully the finish will level out and leave no brush marks. On the other hand, if you fail to follow the instructions unsightly brush marks may appear. The instructions are not complicated.

Basically you have to keep moving to new surfaces as you apply the finish. Apply smoothly but not excessively and move on and the finish will begin leveling within minutes. Never go back over a completed area. The same fast drying that is one of the best features of Deft can be problematic if you go back and brush on an area that has begun to dry. Deft is dry to the touch in under thirty minutes and ready to sand and recoat in about two hours. This means that going back to finished areas will cause ugly brush marks. On the positive side, you could give a project the first coat at noon and be ready for the third coat by 4 p.m.

The one major disadvantage of Deft Clear Wood Finish is its strong odor and vapors. It's critical to either use it in a well ventilated environment or use a good lacquer respirator. One of those cheap respirators used for latex or acrylic paints will not do the job. I sprayed my projects with Deft Clear Wood Finish using a good HVLP (high volume, low pressure) spray unit and always used a respirator. By the way, clean up must be done with lacquer thinner which also has strong odor and vapors and is somewhat expensive compared to paint thinner. It is also highly flammable and should never be used near a flame.

Shopping For Price

Deft has been around and popular for many years so you can find it in many places with varying prices. Shop around for the best price. I could buy it for $20.00 a gallon but often saw it in paint and home improvement stores for as high as $38.00 per gallon. Check local home improvement stores and if you can't find it there for a good price, try department stores like Walmart. I once bought it there for under $20.00 a gallon. I have used Deft for over 25 years and it is one of the best clear products I have ever used.

A Water-based Version

If you don't like the smell and the vapors and prefer a water-based product, Deft Interior Waterborne Clear Wood Finish is a water-based version of their Clear Wood Finish. It also dries fast and levels out well. It looks milky in the container but dries completely clear. Because it is water based, Deft Interior Waterborne Clear Wood Finish has one significant disadvantage when compared to Deft Clear Wood Finish. Like other water based finishes it doesn't function well in colder weather. Once the temperature drops below 65 degrees these finishes begin to act strangely. It doesn't level as well and it takes long periods to dry. Neither is the case with Deft Clear Wood Finish and I have used it in temperatures down to 40 degrees with success. The only real difference was slightly slower drying time.

Bartley's Gel Varnish

Bartley's Gel Varnish is another excellent albeit expensive finish I recommend. It works well and has the rare advantage of not raising the grain of the wood surface. Once you have completed your sanding it may not be necessary to sand between coats. I suggest checking anyway and sanding lightly if it appears necessary. It is a hand rubbed varnish that is applied with a rag or a brush and is more difficult to apply. Also, it has a six-hour drying time so you can't double coat it the same day. Bartley's Gel Varnish comes in clear and in stain colors. The stain colors are a combination of stain and varnish that give an excellent finish. In addition to being more difficult to apply, it does require a lot of rubbing to complete the finish. Once rubbed fully it leaves an excellent, attractive, and highly protected finish.

Staining

I've always preferred natural wood colors but found that most people prefer a stain color. There are many options for stains including oil-based, water-based, and solid stains. The solid stains are sometimes used for furniture because it covers all the defects of natural wood. I prefer using either the oil based or water based stains. There are many brands available so I will only cover the two that I used most often and are readily available in many locations.

Oil Based and Water Based Stains

Deft makes excellent water based stains in many colors and they dry ready for a finish coat within an hour. This fast drying can be a real advantage when used with Deft Clear Wood Finish because it allows you to apply a stain at 10 a.m., apply the first coat of clear before lunch and the last two coats of clear after lunch and the project will be completely dry and ready to move by 4 p.m.

MinWax makes excellent oil based stains which should be allowed to dry overnight before applying a clear coat. It is unwise to rush this process as the stain could run when the clear coat is applied if it has not dried fully. Using products that do not dry rapidly means that your finish job will take two or three days.

Staining Methods

Staining is hard work but it's not difficult to do a good job if you follow certain rules. The most important rule is to apply the stain quickly and evenly. Apply it with the grain of the wood, don't apply with crisscross motions either by hand or with a brush. Never stop in the middle of a section and then come back in a few minutes. The stain in the first section will dry and when you come back you will be applying a second coat that makes that part of the surface look darker. You can avoid this problem by never starting a staining job that you can't complete. The second major rule is to wipe off all the excess stain. The grain of the wood should be clearly visible through the stain without any streaks or heavy patches of stain. Such streaks will get darker and ruin the appearance of the finish. This is the most common mistake in staining.

Wiping Off The Stain

Wiping off the excess stain is a process in itself. With large projects, apply the stain in sections and then wipe off that section before proceeding to the next. A common mistake is allowing the stain to dry longer to make the color darker. While this seems to make sense, it can also cause an uneven color. Always have at least two rags to wipe. One rag is used to clean the excess stain and the other will wipe the surface smooth and even. When the first rag becomes soaked with stain, dispose of it and use the second rag as the first and replace the second rag with a clean rag. Keep up this process until the project is completely stained and wiped.

I suggest you avoid brushing Deft over oil-based stain. The lacquer has a tendency to pull some of the stain off on your brush. It works fine if you are going to spray. For brushing, I suggest a water based MinWax product called Polycrylic. It does an excellent job and dries very fast. Whatever clear coat you use, remember to avoid over brushing and do not go back to surfaces that have already started to dry since this will create deep and unsightly brush marks.

SAFETY NOTE: Dispose of oil-laden rags safely by placing them in a container filled with water. With some oil finishes rags can combust spontaneously and cause a serious fire.

Notes

SAFETY NOTES

POWER TOOLS ARE INHERENTLY DANGEROUS. Any tool that cuts wood can also cut skin and bone. Keep this in mind every time you use a power tool. Plan every cut carefully before starting the tool. Clamp work pieces securely before cutting, routing, sanding or using a Biscuit Joiner. Read and adhere to the safety guidelines that came with the power tool.

These guidelines are written to help you avoid serious injuries. Here are a few more simple hints that will help you avoid injuries. While it is best to use both hands to control power tools, if you are using a power tool with one hand, always check where the other hand is before starting the tool. This may sound silly but it is a good way to keep all your fingers.

Whatever cutting, routing, planing, jointing you are going to do, take a moment to review the procedure in advance. Visualize the complete procedure before you start. Doing this will often allow you to realize mistakes that you may have made without thinking. An extra moment before proceeding could help you avoid potential kickback or other injury causing incidents.

If you believe that these extra precautions are not necessary for you because you are so proficient with the tool, please think again. It does take time to be careful and use power tools safely but not nearly as much time as a serious injury can take out of your life.

Never use power tools if you are tired, taking medications or using alcohol or drugs. This is a sure way to get hurt. Always use ear and eye protection and dust masks when needed. Woodworking is an enjoyable hobby and it can be profitable. Don't let a moment of carelessness ruin it for you. Before turning on any power tool think and make certain you know where both of your hands are. Take good care of yourself and others around you.

BISCUIT JOINER SAFETY

Because the blade is hidden from view except while cutting biscuit slots, the Biscuit Joiner may give a false sense of security. Remember that the small carbide-tipped blade in the Biscuit Joiner is razor sharp and just as capable as any other power saw to injure you if you get careless. All the rules described in this safety section apply fully to the Biscuit Joiner and should be adhered to at all times.

NOTE ON TABLE SAWS

The table saw is probably the most commonly used stationary power tool for woodworking. It is a tool that has many diverse uses. With the right kind of accessories it can perform a wide variety of cuts to help build all kinds of wood projects. It can also be extremely dangerous when used improperly or carelessly as indicated by the fact that more than 90 percent of shop injuries happen while using table saws.

These machines can injure you seriously in various ways. In addition to cutting fingers and hands, large and small pieces of lumber and plywood can be kicked back at you at astounding speed causing serious injury.

Using a table saw, and any other power tool, requires your total attention every minute. Never allow anyone to speak to you while you are using a table saw. If they do, stop the saw immediately before involving yourself in the conversation.

Table saws are intended for use with fences and various guides to control the material in relationship to the cutting blade. It is not a band saw or jig saw that accommodates freehand cutting. Never perform any kind of freehand cuts on a tablesaw. The table saw blade is spinning at over four thousand revolutions per minute and can yank pieces from your hands or kick them back into your face. Every table saw cut should be made using an accessory such as a rip fence, cross cut guide, or some other specially made jig.

This section on safety is not intended to scare you. While I have never suffered a serious injury using woodworking tools, I have seen others hurt causing them immense pain and lost time from work. I want everyone to avoid that experience by understanding the power of these machines.

Be safe while using the Biscuit Joiner or any other power tool by always giving your work on any power tool your full attention. Take the time to learn the safety rules for your machine and adhere to them. It only takes one mistake to cause a serious injury. Please be careful.

Notes

THE PROJECTS

The biscuit joinery methods used for building the projects in this book are applicable to projects of all sizes and levels of complexity. Some of those projects are pictured on the cover and later in this book. I used these methods to build small projects like those in this book and large projects like entire kitchens. However, the projects in this book serve the dual purpose of helping any woodworker to better understand biscuit joinery methods and as good projects for less experienced woodworkers to build for family and friends. The projects are easily built using a small collection of woodworking tools and limited shop space.

All the projects were designed with the goal of being built by one person in one day or one weekend so that I could build them in a few hours during woodworking demonstrations. Following the detailed instructions with each project you should be able to not only build the projects but also learn a great deal about how to take advantage of using the Biscuit Joiner for building many projects.

All the projects are simple yet functional. I built the chair and table many times for my grandchildren and other friends and family. The kitchen range shelf was a popular item on our stove for several years and visitors often asked to buy one for their home. Most of the time I built them as gifts.

Following the instructions you can build them and apply the finish on the same day. Once you have assembled the project, review the section on Finishing as it will help you to apply an attractive finish and tell you about excellent finishing products and methods that you can use to apply three coats of finish in a four hour period.

Well, now you are ready to start. Remember that you can reach me by email at bill@positive-imaging.com . If you want to write me for information, my mailing address is: Bill Benitez; 9016 Palace Parkway; Austin, TX 78748. I appreciate your questions or comments.

PROJECT ONE: CHILD'S HEART CHAIR

Child's Heart Chair Instructions

Materials List: For this project I suggest white pine that is available at most home-improvement stores. You will need only a 5 foot piece of 1 X 12 lumber for the entire project if you layout carefully before cutting. Cut the rectangular pieces to size as listed in the table and then cut them to shape as described in the drawings.

2 - 3/4" X 1 1/2" X 23 1/2"	2 - 3/4" X 1 1/2" X 11 1/4"
2 - 3/4" X 3" X 9"	2 - 3/4" X 3" X 7 1/2"
1 - 3/4" X 10" X 12 1/2"	1 - 3/4" X 9 1/2" X 9"
1 - 3/4" X 5/8" X 9"	2 - 3/4" X 5/8" X 6 1/2"

Cutting the Parts: To cut the parts for this project I used the table saw, circular saw, and jig saw. You can do without the circular saw if your have a full-size table saw. It is difficult to safely crosscut a 1 X 12 on most small bench top table saws.

The first parts cut are the Back and the Seat. Start by cutting them to the proper length. The Seat is 12 1/ 2 inches long and the Back is 9 inches long. Next rip the pieces to the correct width. This is easier to do on a table saw. The Seat is 10 inches wide and the Back will be 9 1/ 2 inches wide but rip it the same width as the Seat to start.

Make a mark 1/ 2 inch in from each end on the back edge of the Seat. Use a straight edge to mark a line from the 1/ 2 inch mark on the back to the front corner. This will give you the angle for the sides of the Seat. Do the same on the other end. Cut this line with the circular saw. You can make certain the cut is straight by clamping a straight edge to the piece before starting the cut. You can also make this cut with a portable jig saw or a band saw if you have one available. With the jig saw or circular saw, clamp the piece to a worktable before beginning the cut. You can also use a taper jig to make these cuts on a table saw if you have one or prefer to make one.

NEVER MAKE FREEHAND CUTS ON THE TABLE SAW. THIS CAN CAUSE KICKBACKS AND SERIOUS INJURIES.

After cutting the angle lines, mark a 1" radius on each of the front corners and cut them with the jig saw. This cut can also be made with a band saw or a scroll saw if you have one. The back corner can be rounded slightly during sanding.

To mark the Back for cutting, start by making a line down the center of the Back from top to bottom. Measure 6 3/ 4 inches from the bottom and mark across the centerline. Using a compass set at 3 inches, make a half circle at the top of the back using the point where the lines cross as the center point. Next, change the compass to 2 inches. Measure 8 3/ 4 inches from the bottom of the Back on each side and make a small mark. Place the point of the compass on the edge of board at the mark and make a 2 inch quarter circle starting at the edge and running until it touches the 3 inch circle. Do the same thing on the other edge. This will give you the shape as shown in the drawing. Print and cut out the full size heart pattern and use it to mark the heart or you can use a piece of carbon paper to transfer the heart to the back. The bottom point of the heart should be 2 inches from the bottom and centered on the centerline. The top of the heart should also be centered on the line. Mark the heart once you have aligned it.

Drill a 5/8 inch hole at the bottom point of the heart making certain the hole is centered with the centerline. The outside diameter of this hole should just touch the inside of the lines. Use the jigsaw to cut out the heart shape and the top curves. Leave the bottom point of the heart rounded so it will be easier to sand and round over with the router.

Next cut the Front and Rear Legs. First rip pieces to 1 1/ 2 inches. Then cut them to length. The Rear Legs are 23 1/ 2 inches long and the Front Legs are 11 1/ 4 inches long. To cut the angle on the top portion of the Rear Legs, make a mark at the top 7/8 inch from the back edge. Measure from the bottom, along the front edge, 13 inches and make another mark. Use a straight edge to mark from the top mark to the bottom mark. This can be cut with the circular saw, jigsaw, or a taper jig on your table saw. Again, clamp the pieces to the table for cutting.

Now cut the Support pieces. First rip them to 3 inches wide and then cut them to length. The Front and Back Supports are 9 inches long and the Side Supports are 7 1/ 2 inches long. Here you have a choice to make. You can leave the Supports plain or cut hearts in them. I chose to cut the hearts on the side pieces and a pattern for the heart is included. Make a centerline vertically and horizontally and center the heart pattern over it. Mark the heart in the center of both of the Side Supports. Cut the heart by drilling a 1/ 2 inch hole at the bottom point and two 3/ 4 inch holes to form the top part of the heart. Finish the heart by cutting between the holes with a jigsaw.

The final pieces to cut are the Seat Strips. These may be cut from scrap. Rip them to 5/8 inch using the table saw. Be sure to use a push stick when ripping pieces this thin.

KEEP YOUR FINGERS AWAY FROM THE BLADE. After ripping, cut pieces to length. Two of the pieces are 9 inches long and two are 6 1/ 2 inches long.

Sanding: With the exception of the Seat Strips, all the parts should be sanded before assembly. Start by sanding all the edges with a belt sander using a fine grit belt. All the faces of the parts should be sanded with a random orbit sander or a finish sander. The inside of the hearts can be sanded with a small sanding drum attached to your drill. I suggest a 5/8 inch drum. These are available at most home improvement stores. Complete all the sanding at this stage because it is always easier to sand prior to assembly.

Biscuit Layout and Cutting: The first step is to layout the biscuit slot locations. Mark the center of each biscuit as shown on the plans. Remember that you must mark both pieces that correspond to each other. The location of the biscuit slots is not critical as long as the two pieces that go together are marked in alignment with each other. The Side Support goes flush with the top of the Front Leg. Mark the location of the biscuits at the center of all the Supports. This is 1 1/ 2 inch from the edge. Measure 1 1/ 2 inch down the inside front edge of each Front Leg for the location of the biscuit slots. To mark the location of the Side Supports on the rear legs, place the Front Leg against the rear leg and mark at the top edge. If you prefer, just measure up 11 1/ 4 inch from the bottom of the Rear Leg for this mark. Lay one Rear Leg, one Front Leg and a Side Support flat on your worktable as shown on the drawings. Now transfer the biscuit marks from the Side Supports to the Front and Rear Legs. Repeat that procedure with the other Legs and Side Support.

Now mark the biscuit slot locations on the Back by measuring 1 3/ 4 inch from the top and the bottom on each side. Make your marks on the face of the Back. Lay the two Rear Legs on your work bench with the back edge down and make a mark on the inside of each one 2 inches from the top. Place the back between the Legs using the 2 inch marks to properly align it.

Transfer the biscuit marks to the inside front edge of the Rear Legs. The bottom edge of the Back Support is located 6 1/ 2 inches from the bottom of the Rear Legs. Place the Back Support at this location and carry the biscuit marks over to the inside back edge of the Rear Legs.

Now you are ready to cut the slots. The slots are cut with a Biscuit Joiner. The Biscuit Joiner has a fence to control the location of the slot. Set the fence to 5/16 inch for the first cuts. Clamp the Back face up on the table. Make certain that the side edge overhangs the table. Now place the fence of the biscuit joiner squarely on the face of the back and line it up with the slot marks. Make both cuts and then turn the Back around and repeat the procedure to cut the slots on the other side.

Follow the same procedure with the support pieces making certain that every piece is clamped on the table with the face up to ensure proper alignment. Without changing the setting on the biscuit joiner, cut the slots on the front edge of the Rear Legs and the back edge of the Front Legs. Remember to clamp the pieces down to cut them and make certain that the face is up when it is clamped. After you have finished these cuts, readjust the biscuit joiner fence to 7/16 inch and make the slots on the inside of the Front and Rear Legs including the slots for the Back. This adjustment will recess the Back and the Supports 1/8 inch. With all the biscuit slots cut you are ready for assembly.

Note: Remember that you can make all of these same cuts without using the fence, as I prefer to do when possible, by simply using the workbench top as the fence for your cuts. Then with the front leg cuts, instead of readjusting the fence you can use a 1/8 inch filler to raise the Biscuit Joiner and change the location of the slot.

Optional Routing: As a decorative option you can rout some of the edges with a 1/ 4 inch round over bit. I suggest that you rout both sides of the heart and the top and bottom edge of the Back. Also rout the face side of the hearts in the Supports. Finally, rout the top and bottom edges of the front and both sides of the Seat. Sand all the routed edges before assembly.

Assembly: Start by assembling the two sides. Hold the Support piece with one hand and squeeze a little glue across the inside of both sides of the biscuit slot. Make these beads of glue narrow because too much glue will just ooze out and make a mess. Place a biscuit in the glued slot and tap it in as necessary with a mallet. If in doubt, use a small art brush to spread the glue in the slot. Repeat the procedure on the other end. Now glue up the slot on the Rear Leg and slide the proper biscuit into the slot. Glue up the slot in the Front Leg and slide it over the other biscuit making certain that the pieces are correctly assembled as shown in the drawing. Now clamp the three pieces together and repeat the entire procedure with the pieces for the other side of the chair. While these are drying, glue up and install biscuits in the slots on the Front and Back Supports and the Back.

After about two hours, unclamp the side pieces. Proceed by gluing up the slots on one side and installing the Back, the Front Support and the Back Support. Quickly glue up the slots on the other side, gently pick up the partial assembly and insert the biscuits into the slots on the other side. Now, stand the assembly upright, check the alignment of all the parts, and clamp the sides tightly to the Supports and the Back making certain that none of the joints are loose. Make certain that the Legs are all flat on the bench. If they aren't, move the clamps slightly to change the pressure points until the Legs do set flat. Next use a small square to check the squareness of the chair. If it is not square, use a clamp diagonally to bring it into square. Allow the glue to dry for at least one hour before taking the clamps off. Once the glue has dried, remove the clamps. Now you can install the Seat.

Start by preparing the Seat Strips. Drill 3/16 inch holes in the Seat Strips as shown in the drawings. You will need two holes to fasten the Strips to the chair frame and two holes to fasten the Seat. The holes should be reamed out slightly to accommodate the head of the screws. Use 1 1/ 4 inch drywall screws and a little glue to fasten the seat strips to the chair Supports. The screws should go through the 3/ 4 inch thickness into the chair. Once all three Strips are attached place the Seat over the Strips and align it as shown on the drawing. Now drive screws in from the bottom into the Seat to hold it in place. Do not glue the seat on.

Finishing: Sand the entire chair by hand or with an orbital sander using 220-grit sandpaper. Clean all the dust off, first with a rag and then with a tack cloth. If you want a darker color, apply a stain of your choice. Remember that stains must be wiped thoroughly until all the streaks are gone and the grain is clear. Allow the stain to dry and then apply 2 or 3 coats of varnish, polyurethane, or Deft, sanding with 400-grit sandpaper between each coat. The finished chair should have a very smooth finish. As an added decoration, a small cushion can be made for the seat in the color of your choice.

CHILD'S CHAIR DRAWINGS

Drawings are not to scale. Use listed dimensions

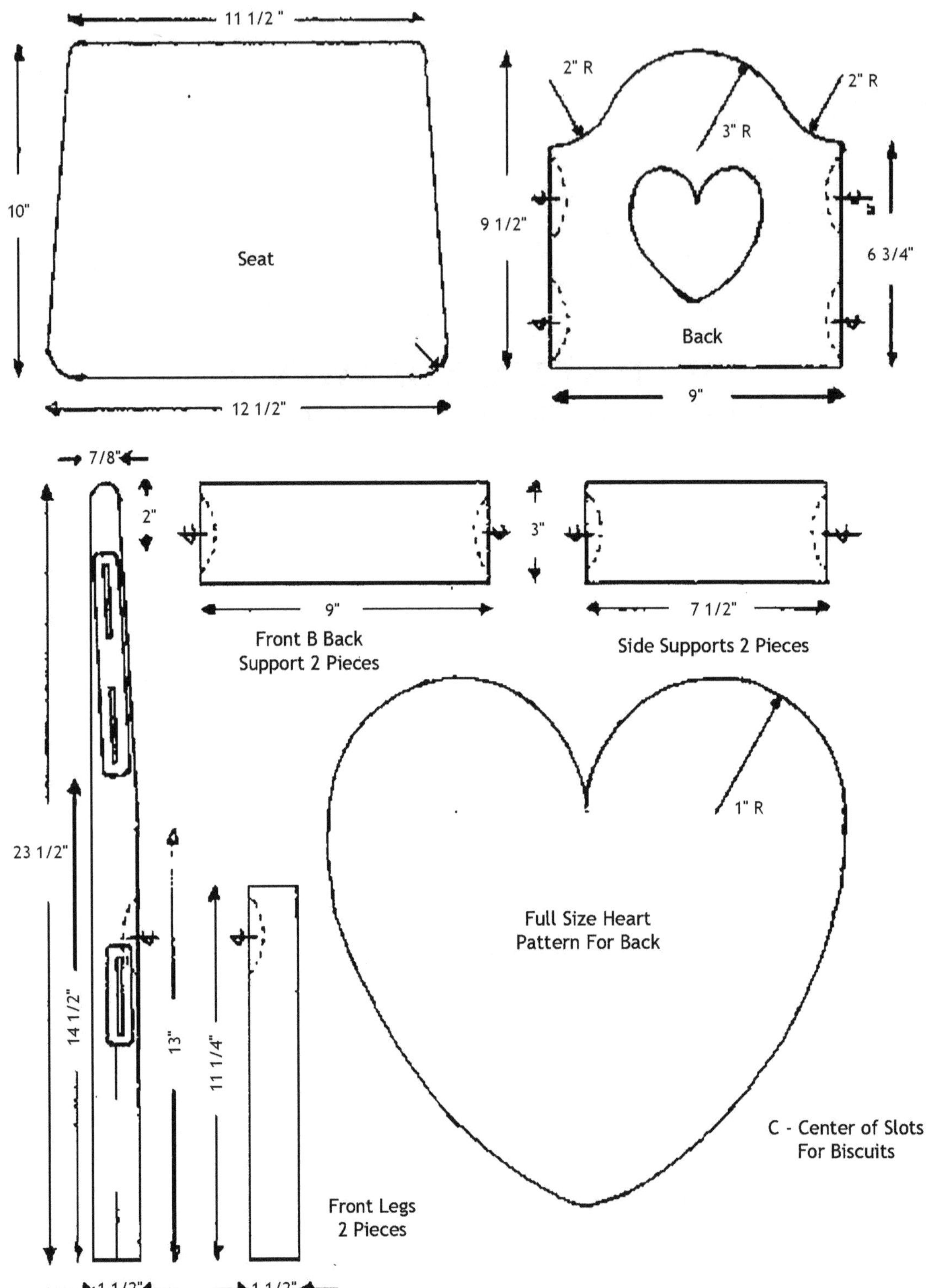
11 1/2"
10"
Seat
12 1/2"
2" R
2" R
3" R
9 1/2"
6 3/4"
Back
9"
7/8"
2"
3"
9"
Front B Back
Support 2 Pieces
7 1/2"
Side Supports 2 Pieces
1" R
23 1/2"
14 1/2"
13"
11 1/4"
Full Size Heart
Pattern For Back
C - Center of Slots
For Biscuits
Front Legs
2 Pieces
1 1/2"
1 1/2"

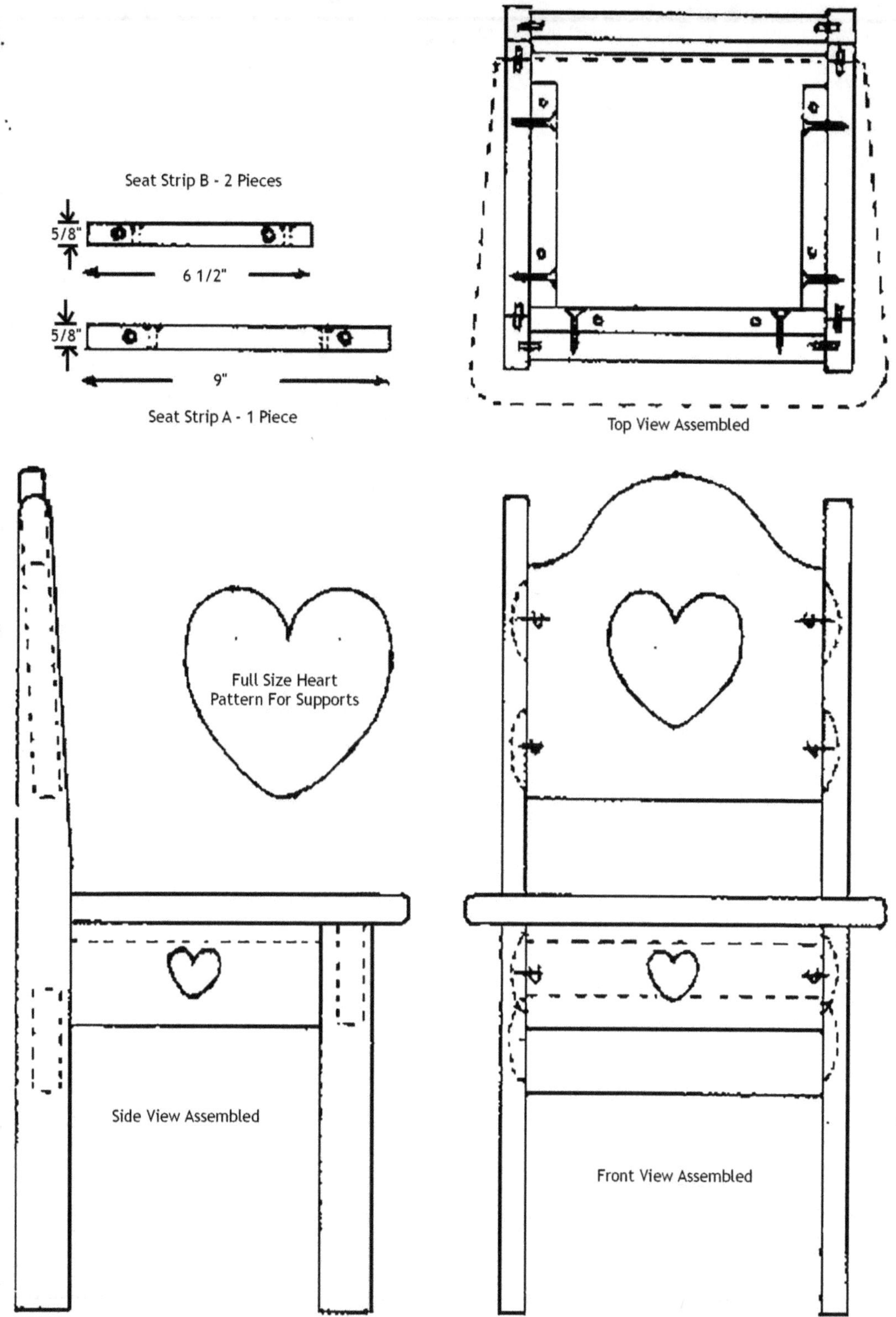
Seat Strip B - 2 Pieces
5/8"
6 1/2"
5/8"
9"
Seat Strip A - 1 Piece
Top View Assembled
Full Size Heart Pattern For Supports
Side View Assembled
Front View Assembled

Notes

PROJECT TWO: BOOKCASE

Bookcase Instructions

Materials List: For this project I suggest white pine because it is readily available. You will need only one 6 foot piece and one 8 foot piece of 1 X 8 for the entire project if you layout carefully before cutting. All the dimensions are clearly described in the drawings. Just cut the following rectangular pieces and then cut the shapes as described in the next section.

2 - 3/4" X 7 1/4" X 35 1/2"

4 - 3/4" X 7" X 16 1/2"

1 - 3/4" X 2 1/2" X 16 1/2"

1 - 3/4" X 3 1/2" X 16 1/2"

Cutting the Parts: I used only the table saw and the jigsaw to cut this project. The first parts cut were the Sides. The Sides are left at the full 1 X 8 width which is about 7 1/ 4 inches and are cut to 35 1/ 2 inches long. Cut the Shelves to 16 1/ 2 inches long and then rip them to 7 inches. Cut five Shelves, which is one extra, but only rip the four that will be used as Shelves for the project. The fifth piece will be cut for the Top Decorative Support and the Toe Board.

Draw the Decorative Support board using a compass. Notice on the drawings the position of the centers for your compass. Start by finding the center of the board and making a line squarely across it. Measure from the bottom 2 1/ 2 inches and make a cross mark. Now set the compass to 1 1/ 4 inch and make a complete circle using the center mark. Next measure up 4 1/ 2 inches from the bottom, on both ends of the board. Draw a line squarely at least 2 inches into the board at each end. Now, measure 2 inches along this line and make a cross mark. This is your center. Set your compass to 3 inches and make a half circle from the outside edge of the board toward the center on both ends. Now clamp the board to your table and extend the centerline that you made down at least 5 inches below the board. Measure up the centerline on the board 3 1/ 2 inches and make a mark. From that mark, measure down below the board 8 inches and make a cross mark. This is the center for the final marks. Set your compass to 8 inches. If your compass is not large enough you can simply improvise one using a pencil with a short string tied to it. Place a nail on the center mark and tie the string to the pencil and the nail setting the length at 8 inches. Draw a partial circle from one of the 3 inch radiuses to the other. Erase all the excess marks to avoid mistakes when cutting. Before cutting the Decorative Support, cut the Toe Board by ripping off the top portion of the board at 2 1/ 2 inches. This will make the cutting of the Decorative support easier. Cut the Decorative Support using a jigsaw. Next mark the 2 1/ 2 inch radiuses on the top end of the Sides and cut them with the jigsaw.

Before proceeding to the next step sand all the edges that will be exposed. This includes all the jigsaw cuts on the Sides and the Decorative Support and the ripped edge of all the Shelves. Sanding edges is best done with a belt sander. Clamp each work piece tightly before you sand the edges. The inside radiuses can be sanded with a small drum sanding attachment used on a drill.

Biscuit Layout and Cutting: Start the layout for the biscuit slots by placing the Sides back edge to back edge with the tops flush and the outside faces down on the table. The drawings show the exact location of the Shelves on each Side. To layout simply begin measuring from the bottom. Measure from the bottom 2 1/ 2 inches and mark a square line across both Sides. Next measure up 12 inches and mark another square line. Third measure 8 3/ 4 inches and mark a square line and finally measure another 8 3/ 4 inches and mark a square line across both Sides. The lines you have marked indicate the bottom of each Shelf.

In the interest of clarity I would advise you to mark one or two small X marks on the topside of each Shelf line so you will remember what side of the line the Shelf goes. Now mark each Shelf on each end on the top surface to show the center of each biscuit slot. Measure 1 1/ 2 inch and 5 1/ 4 inches from the back edge of each Shelf and make a mark on the ends, top face, of every Shelf. By making all the marks the same it is unnecessary to identify the location of each Shelf because they will fit on any of the layout lines.

Remove the fence from your Biscuit Joiner or fold it back out of the way depending on the model. Set the biscuit slot depth for a size 20 biscuit. Follow the instructions with your biscuit joiner to do this. Now start with the first Side and place the first Shelf back edge flush with the back edge of the Side, the bottom of the Shelf should be flat on the inside of the Side, and the end of the shelf precisely on the line. Clamp the two pieces together on your worktable. Place the Biscuit Joiner upright with the base against the edge of the Shelf and the face against the inside of the Side. Center the guideline on the bottom of the Biscuit Joiner with the mark you made on the Shelf making certain that the biscuit joiner base is tight against the Shelf edge and the face is lying flat on the Side, then cut both biscuit slots. Now turn your biscuit joiner around so the face is against the Shelf edge and the base is lying flat on the inside of the Side. Make certain the biscuit joiner guideline is aligned with the marks on the Shelf and cut the slots. Next, unclamp the Shelf. Clamp the next Shelf on the second line and repeat the process until you have done all four Shelves.

After you have completed all the shelves on one side, repeat this procedure on the other Side cutting the slots on the opposite end of each Shelf and on the other Side. Remember to make certain each piece is properly oriented before making each cut.

Layout the biscuit slots for the Decorative Support and the Toe Board. First mark on the back of the Decorative Support by measuring 1 inch from the bottom on each end and making a mark. Then mark on the back bottom edge of the Decorative Support at 3 inches from each side and at the center that is 8 1/ 4 inch. Now mark the face of the Toe Board at 1 1/ 4 inch from the bottom on each end. Transfer the end marks on the Toe Board to the bottom, front edge of each Side. Transfer the marks on the bottom edge of the Decorative Support to the top, back edge of the Shelf that will be used as the top Shelf. Transfer the marks on the ends of the Decorative Support to the top, back edge of the Sides. This mark can best be done by measuring 1 3/ 4 inches up from the line of the top Shelf. This will be the Shelf thickness of 3/ 4 inch plus the 1 inch to the mark on the Decorative Support.

Reinstall the fence on your biscuit joiner and change the setting for size 0 biscuits. Be sure to set the fence to 5\16 inch on the gauge at the face of your biscuit joiner. Now clamp the Decorative Support face down on your worktable with the end overhanging. Place the biscuit joiner with the fence on the back of the Decorative Support and the guide line on the mark and cut the slot making certain that the fence is flat with the back of the Decorative Support. Now clamp the Decorative Support with the other end overhanging and repeat the process. Clamp the Decorative Support so that the back edge is overhanging and cut the three slots on the bottom edge. Next clamp the Toe Board face up with the end overhanging and use the marks to make the slots on both ends of the Toe Board.

To cut the aligning slots on the Sides and the top Shelf, clamp the first Side on your work table with the top back overhanging to accommodate the fence. Remember that all the cuts are on the inside surface of the Sides. Place the Biscuit Joiner face on the inside of the Side and the fence against the back edge of the Side and align the guideline with the mark. The biscuit joiner will be upright for this cut. Make certain the biscuit joiner face is flat on the Side and make the cut. Now clamp down the other Side in the same manner and make the other cut. Clamp the top Shelf on the worktable face up with the back edge overhanging. Place the face of the biscuit joiner on the top of the Shelf with the fence against the back edge and the guideline aligned with the first mark. Making certain the biscuit joiner face is flat with the Shelf top, make the first cut. Move the Biscuit Joiner and make the second and third cuts.

In order to have a 1 inch set back of the Toe Board, you must set the fence of your biscuit joiner to the 1 5\16 inch mark before making the cut for the Toe Board on the Side. Clamp the Side so the bottom front edge is overhanging and the inside is up. Now place the Biscuit Joiner face on the inside of the Side and the fence on the front edge with the guideline aligned with the mark. Make the cut after making certain that the face of the Biscuit Joiner is flat with the Side. Repeat the process with the other Side and you have completed cutting all the biscuit slots.

Routing the Edges: For the inside of the Sides and the bottom of the Shelves use the 1/ 4 inch round over router bit set flush with the base of your router or your router table if you have mounted your router on a table. This project can be done either way, but with small work it is usually best to mount your router in a router table. Start by testing the setting of your router bit on a scrap piece of lumber. If the cut isn't right make the necessary adjustment and test again. Now round over the inside edge, front and top of each Side, then round over the bottom edge, front only, of all the Shelves. Now reset the depth of the 1/ 4 inch round over bit. Set it to cut deeper thereby forming a bead approximately 1\16 inch high. Once again test the cut to make certain you are getting what you want. Then rout the outside of the Sides, front and top only. Next, rout the front of each Shelf. Finally, rout the top edge only of the Decorative Support following the curves. Move the router slowly as you rout the area near the center circle. This area has a couple of points that could break off if pushed too hard. Make certain your router bit is sharp. It is always preferable to use a carbide-tipped router bit.

Sanding: It is always easier to sand project parts prior to assembly. Use a random orbit or an orbital sander with 120-grit sandpaper to clean up all the imperfections on the surfaces and to remove all the pencil marks you made for cutting the biscuit slots. These marks are no longer needed. Also hand sand all the round overs that you routed as necessary. For the most part, these round overs will be smooth enough but when you rout across the grain it tends to get rough. Sand these areas to ensure a smooth finished product.

Assembly: Assembling a project using biscuits requires a little planning. If you don't plan the process you may wind up placing glue in a biscuit slot and having to turn the piece upside down allowing the glue to flow out and make a mess. The first step with the assembly of this project is to assemble the Decorative Support to the top Shelf. Start by putting glue in the slots on the bottom edge of the Decorative Support. Remember to use the glue sparingly. Use a glue bottle tip that has a small round opening and run a thin bead of glue just inside each slot on both sides. If you have done this properly the slot will not fill up and the glue will not ooze out when you insert the biscuit. If the glue oozes out you are using too much glue. Lighten up before continuing. You can also use a small art brush to smooth out the glue in the slot before inserting the biscuit. Make certain that the biscuits are completely inserted by tapping them with a mallet. Next place the top Shelf face up on your worktable and put glue in the three slots. Now align the biscuits on the bottom edge of the Decorative support with the slots and tap the pieces together. Remember not to tap near the center because the decorative points are vulnerable. Clamp the two pieces together with two clamps making certain that the joint closes tightly and the ends are aligned.

Now you are ready to assemble the bookcase. To avoid making a glue mess, place all the biscuits on one of the two Sides and on the opposite ends of every Shelf, the Decorative Support and the Toe Board. The simplest way to do this without making a mistake is to place one Side inside up on your worktable. Now put glue in the glue slots and insert all the biscuits. After you have inserted all the biscuits on the first Side, place each Shelf where it belongs without glue in the matching slot. This is just a dry test to make certain you place the biscuits in the correct order. Also place the Decorative Support with the Shelf and the Toe Board in place. Now, put glue in the exposed slots and insert the biscuits into the ends of these parts as you did into the Side.

Once you have completed this process you are ready to assemble the project without making a glue mess. Remove the parts from the Side with the biscuits inserted. Replace the Side on the worktable with the Side that has no biscuits. Now put glue in these biscuit slots and insert the shelf ends with the biscuits into the slots on the Side. Do this rapidly because the biscuits will begin to swell the minute they touch the glue. Once you have inserted and aligned all the parts, put glue in all the exposed slots again. This time the slots will be on the ends of the Shelves, the Decorative Support and the Toe Board. Now place the Side with the biscuits inserted over these parts and align the biscuits with the slots forcing them in with light taps with a mallet. Once the joints close stand the Bookcase upright and clamp the Sides together using at least 6 clamps; 3 on the front edge and 3 on the back edge. These clamps are placed at the top, bottom and center making certain all the joints are tightly closed. If you are using metal clamps be sure to place scrap wood pieces between the clamp and the wood surfaces to avoid marring. While the glue is still wet, lay the bookcase face down on your work table and check the back edge of your Bookcase to make certain that the Shelves are flush with the Sides. If they aren't quite flush, loosen the clamps slightly and tap the shelves with a mallet until they are flush. Then retighten the clamps.

Check that the bookcase is square. This is easy to do with a large metal square or by measuring the diagonals. Simply use your tape to measure on the back of the project, from the top right hand corner to the bottom left hand corner. Then measure from the top left hand corner to the bottom right hand corner. If your project is square these dimensions will be identical. If they aren't, you must use a long clamp on the longest diagonal to draw the project square.

Sometimes you can make a project square by merely realigning your clamps. Always try to place your clamps at a 90-degree angle to avoid pulling things out of square. After the project is square, allow the glue to dry for at least two hours before removing the clamps. Your project is now complete except for the finish.

Finishing: Sand the entire project lightly with 220-grit sandpaper either by hand or with an orbital sander. This is a very light sanding since you already sanded all the surfaces before assembly. If you want a darker color than the natural wood, apply a stain. Follow the instructions on the stain can but remember that stains must be wiped off thoroughly to remove all streaks.

Allow the stain to dry overnight and then apply 2 or 3 coats of varnish, polyurethane or Deft. Sand by hand with 400-grit sandpaper between coats to ensure a very smooth final finish. I suggest you use a satin or semi-gloss clear finish for a smooth rich furniture look.

Assembly Options: Most simplified woodworking projects are assembled with biscuits using a Biscuit Joiner. I do this because biscuits are the simplest, strong method of assembly. It is not the only method and you always have options. That is especially so with this project. The bookcase can be assembled using screws with plugs. Another option is to use trim screws that have a head slightly larger that a finish nail. With these you can use wood filler to fill the holes. You can also consider making the bookcase rustic or primitive and not filling in the screw holes at all. This is not unusual and furniture of this kind can be found at many stores selling country furniture. You can even make dado cuts for the shelves or use dowels, even though it would make the job much more difficult and time consuming. In all simplified woodworking projects, the objective is simplicity but there are always options open to you. After all, this is your project. Be creative and build it the way you choose.

Notes

BOOKCASE DRAWINGS

Drawings are not to scale. Use listed dimensions

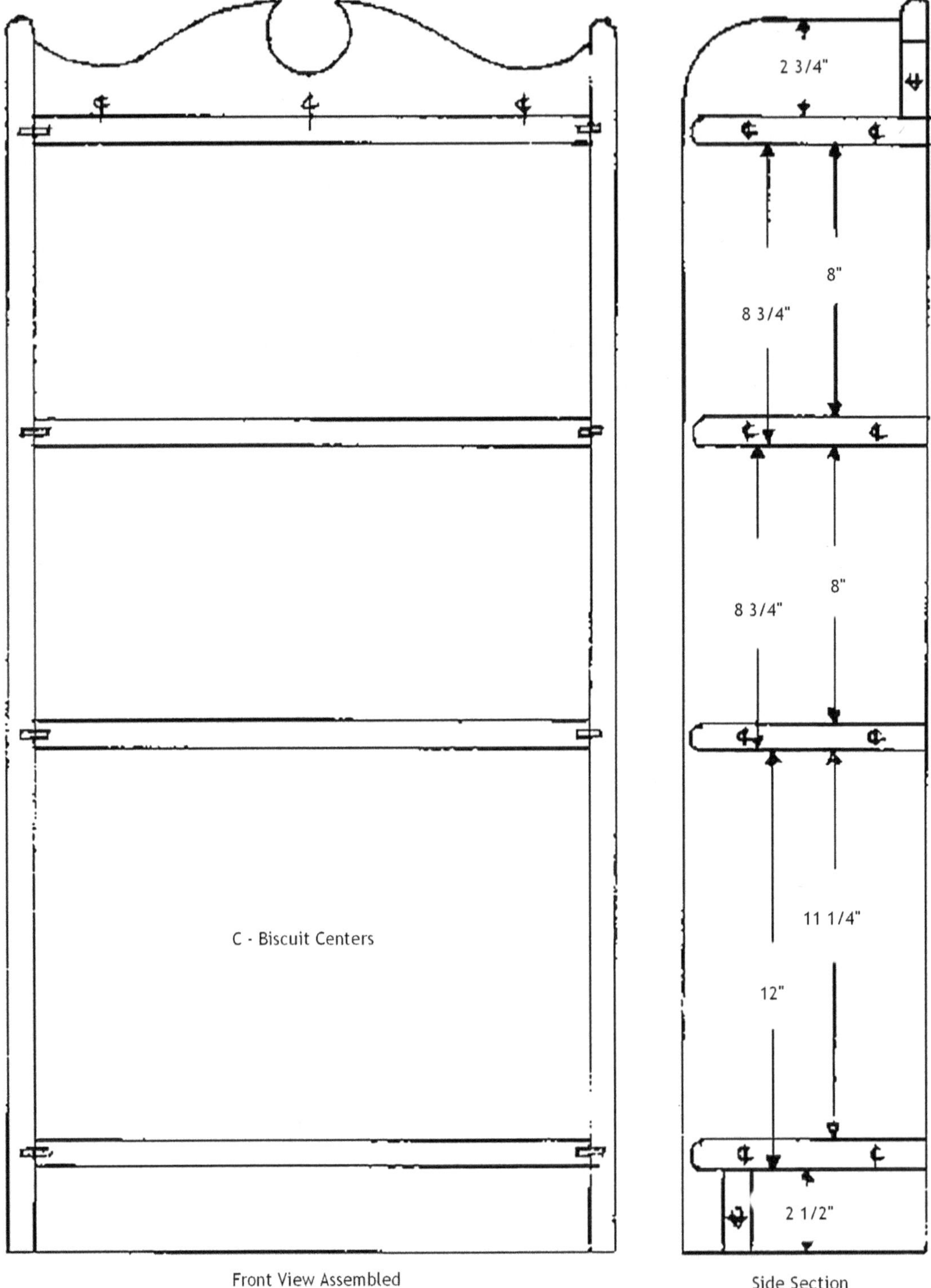

Front View Assembled

Side Section

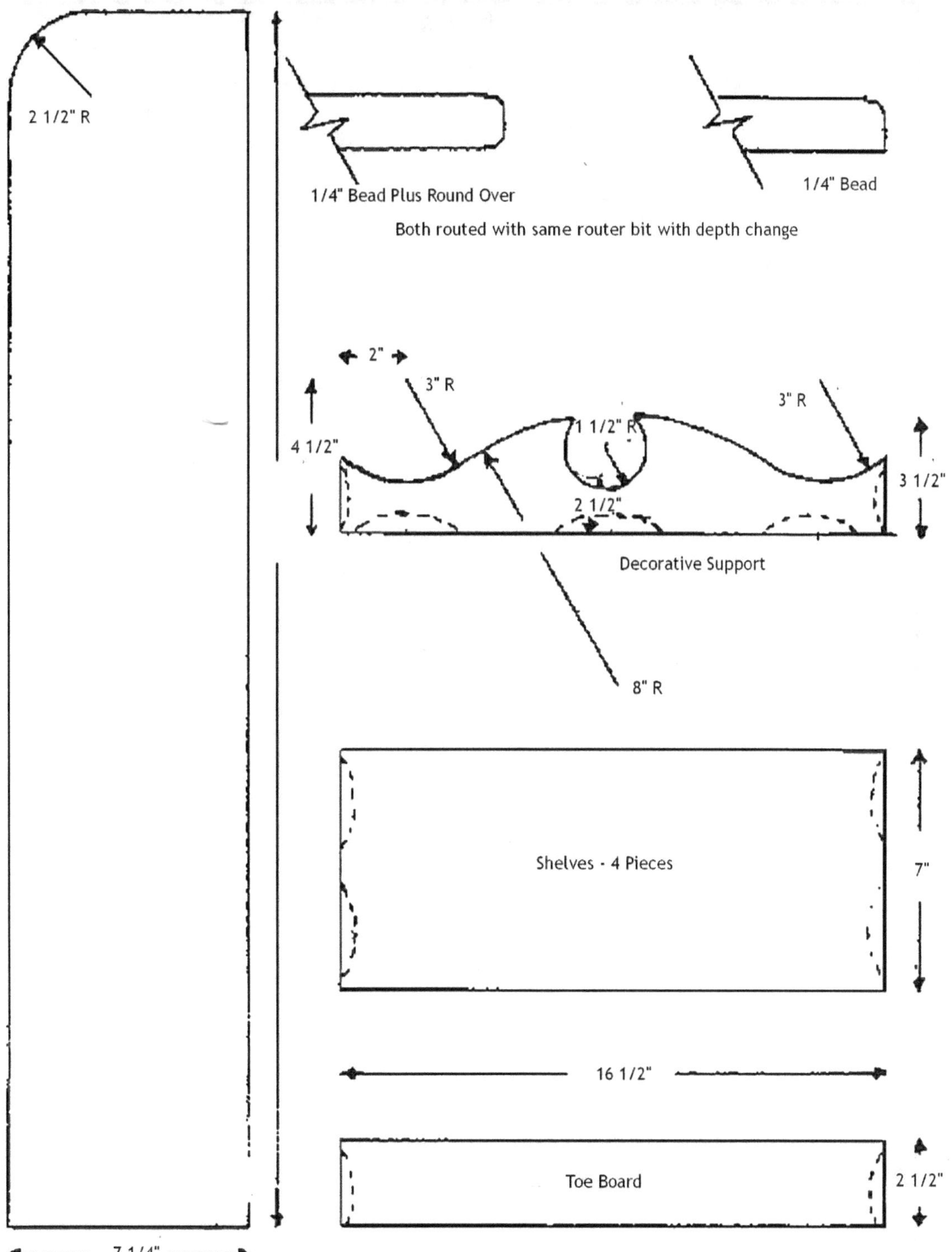
2 1/2" R
1/4" Bead Plus Round Over
1/4" Bead
Both routed with same router bit with depth change
2"
3" R
3" R
4 1/2"
1 1/2" R
2 1/2"
3 1/2"
Decorative Support
8" R
Shelves - 4 Pieces
7"
16 1/2"
Toe Board
2 1/2"
7 1/4"

Notes

PROJECT THREE: KITCHEN RANGE SHELF

Kitchen Range Shelf Instructions

Materials List: For this project I suggest using wood that matches your kitchen cabinets. You will need only one 8 foot piece of 1 X 10 for the entire project if you layout carefully before cutting. All the dimensions are clearly described in the drawings. Just cut the following rectangular pieces and then cut the shapes as described in the next section.

1 - 3/4" X 6" X 29 1/4"   1 - 3/4" X 8 1/4" X 30"

2 - 3/4" X 3" X 8"

Cutting the Parts: I used the table saw and the jigsaw to cut the pieces for this project. The first step is to cross cut all the pieces. Cut the first piece 30 inches long. This is the Back. Cut the piece for the Base 29 1/ 4 inches long. Cut the pieces for the two Top Shelves 8 inches long. Next rip the parts to the correct width. The Back is ripped to 8 1/ 4 inches. The Base is ripped to 6 inches and the Top Shelves are ripped to 3 inches. Use a compass to layout the radiuses shown on the drawings. First layout the Back by measuring in from each end 10 1/ 2 inches and drawing a square line about 4 inches into the board. Now measure up from the bottom 4 inches and mark a straight line from one of the 10 1/ 2 inch marks to the other. Measure in toward the center from each 10 1/ 2 inch mark 2 inches and make a mark. Now measure up from the 4 inch line 2 inches and make a mark to cross the other 2 inch mark. This is the center point for the inside radiuses.

Measure 1 inch in from each side of each corner as shown on the plan to mark the center of the other four radiuses on the Back. Next, do the same to both front corners of the Base and both front corners of the Top Shelves. Use the jigsaw with a fine tooth blade to cut all the radiuses and to cut out the center section of the Back. You can also use a band saw or scroll saw to make these cuts. Sand all the edges using a belt sander and a small drum sander on your drill to get the inside radiuses.

Biscuit Layout and Cutting: Start the layout for the biscuit slots by placing the Back face up on your table. Now place the Base in its proper location with the bottom of the Base flush with the bottom edge of the Back. Clamp these together temporarily. Now mark the location of the biscuit centers on the bottom edge of the Back and the bottom side of the Base and unclamp them. Now draw a line 2 inches from the top edge of the Back all the way across. This will place the top of the Shelf 1 1/ 4 inch from the top edge of the Back. This is the location of the Top Shelves. Also make a mark 1 1/ 4 inch in from each side and in from the center. This will indicate the location of the Top Shelves side to side. Now mark the biscuit slot centers on the top of the Shelves.

Set your Biscuit Joiner for size 20 biscuits. Adjust the fence on your Biscuit Joiner to 1\4 inch from the blade line. Clamp the Base face down on your table with the back edge overhanging. Place the Biscuit Joiner fence flat on the bottom of the Base and align the guideline of the Biscuit Joiner with the first mark. Making certain that the fence remains completely flat with the bottom edge of the Base, cut all five biscuit slots carefully. If you own a portable workbench or a woodworkers vise, clamp the Back in it, upside down and with the face to you. This will make the biscuit slot center marks visible to you. You can also clamp the Back face up on your workbench with the bottom edge overhanging. Place the Biscuit Joiner fence carefully on the bottom edge of the Back. Make certain that the fence is flat on the bottom edge and the face of the Biscuit Joiner is flat on the face of the Back. Cut the biscuit slot and repeat the procedure carefully for all the biscuit slots.

For the next step you must remove the fence from your Biscuit Joiner or fold it up. Place the Back face up on your workbench with the top edge overhanging. Place the two Top Shelves face up on the face of the Back. These shelves must be placed with the back/bottom edge flush with the Top Shelf location lines on the Back. Clamp the two Top Shelves onto the Back. Now place the Biscuit Joiner upright with the base against the back edge of the Top Shelf and the face against the Back. Make certain the Biscuit Joiner guideline is aligned with the mark on the top face of the Top Shelf and cut the slot. Repeat this process for both biscuit slots on both Top Shelves.

Next turn the Biscuit Joiner so the base is flat on the face of the Back and the face of the Biscuit Joiner is flat against the back edge of the Top Shelf. Align the guideline with the mark and cut both slots in both Top Shelves. Remove the clamps and you are ready for assembly.

Routing the Edges: Routing the edges requires only one router bit. For all the routing I used a 1/ 4 inch round over bit. I set the router up on a router table and then set the bit about 1\16 inch above the table to add a slight bead to the cut. Once the router table is set up, run a test piece to make certain the cut is what you want. Always test before cutting the actual work piece. Then rout the front and side edges of the Top Shelves and the Base, making certain that the cut is made on the top or face side. The Back is only routed on the sides, top, and center, also on the front or face side. Remember to take special precautions when routing small pieces such as the top shelves.

Sanding: It is always easier to sand project parts prior to assembly. Use a random orbit sander or an orbital sander with 120-grit sandpaper to clean up all the imperfections on the surfaces and remove all the pencil marks you made for cutting the biscuit slots. These marks are no longer needed. Also hand sand all the round overs that you routed. For the most part these round overs will be smooth enough but when you rout across the grain it tends to get rough. Sand all the rough areas to ensure a smooth finished product.

Assembly: This is a very easy project to assemble. Nevertheless, it is important to plan the assembly before proceeding. Using biscuits requires a little planning because you can easily place glue in a biscuit slot and then have to turn the part upside down allowing the glue to flow out and make a mess. Remember to use the glue sparingly. Most people use too much glue on woodworking projects. This creates a difficult clean up situation and a problem for your finish.

Start the assembly process by placing glue in the biscuit slots on the back of the Top Shelves and the back of the Base. Then insert the biscuits and tap them in with a mallet. Now lay the Back, face up, on the worktable and place glue in the biscuit slots. First, glue up the slots along the bottom edge. Then promptly insert the biscuits on the Base into the biscuit slots on the bottom edge of the Back. Use the mallet to tap the biscuits into place. Make certain the Base is centered on the back. Next place glue in the biscuit slots along the top of the Back. Now insert the biscuits on the back of each Shelf and adjust them to the right location. Tap the Top Shelves in with the mallet. Then check the 1 1/ 4 inch measurement to make certain the Top Shelves are in the right position. Quickly clamp all the pieces together tightly and check that they remain square with the Back. Use a small square to check this squareness. If it isn't quite square, adjust the clamps so the pieces wind up square. Once the glue dries remove the clamps and proceed to the finishing.

Finishing: Sand the entire project lightly with 220-grit sandpaper, either by hand or with an orbital sander. This is a very light sanding since you already sanded all the surfaces before assembly. If you want a darker color than the natural wood, apply a stain of your choice. Follow the instructions on the stain can but remember that stains must be wiped off thoroughly to remove all streaks. Allow the stain to dry overnight and then apply 2 or 3 coats of varnish, polyurethane or Deft. Sand by hand with 400-grit sandpaper between coats to ensure a very smooth final finish. I suggest using satin or semi-gloss clear finish for a smooth, rich furniture look.

Assembly Options: Most simplified woodworking projects are assembled with biscuits using a Biscuit Joiner . I do this because biscuits are the simplest, strong method of assembly. It is not the only method and you always have options. The Kitchen Range Shelf can be assembled using screws from the back since they will not be visible after installation. In all simplified woodworking projects, there are always options open to you. After all, this is your project. Be creative and build it your way.

KITCHEN RANGE SHELF DRAWINGS

Drawings are not to scale. Use listed dimensions

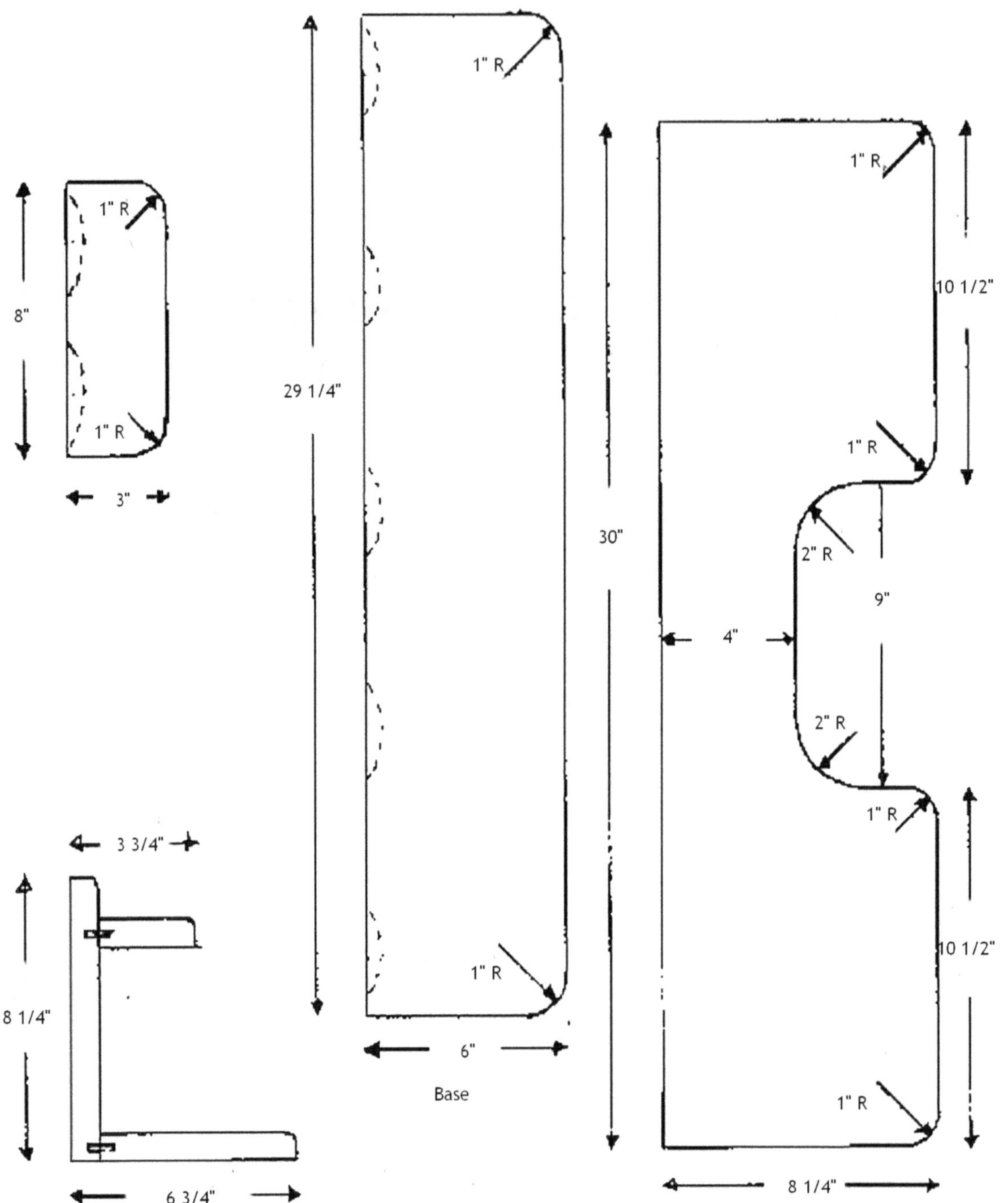
1" R
1" R
8"
3"
1" R
29 1/4"
1" R
6"
Base
3 3/4"
8 1/4"
6 3/4"
1" R
10 1/2"
30"
1" R
2" R
9"
4"
2" R
1" R
10 1/2"
1" R
8 1/4"

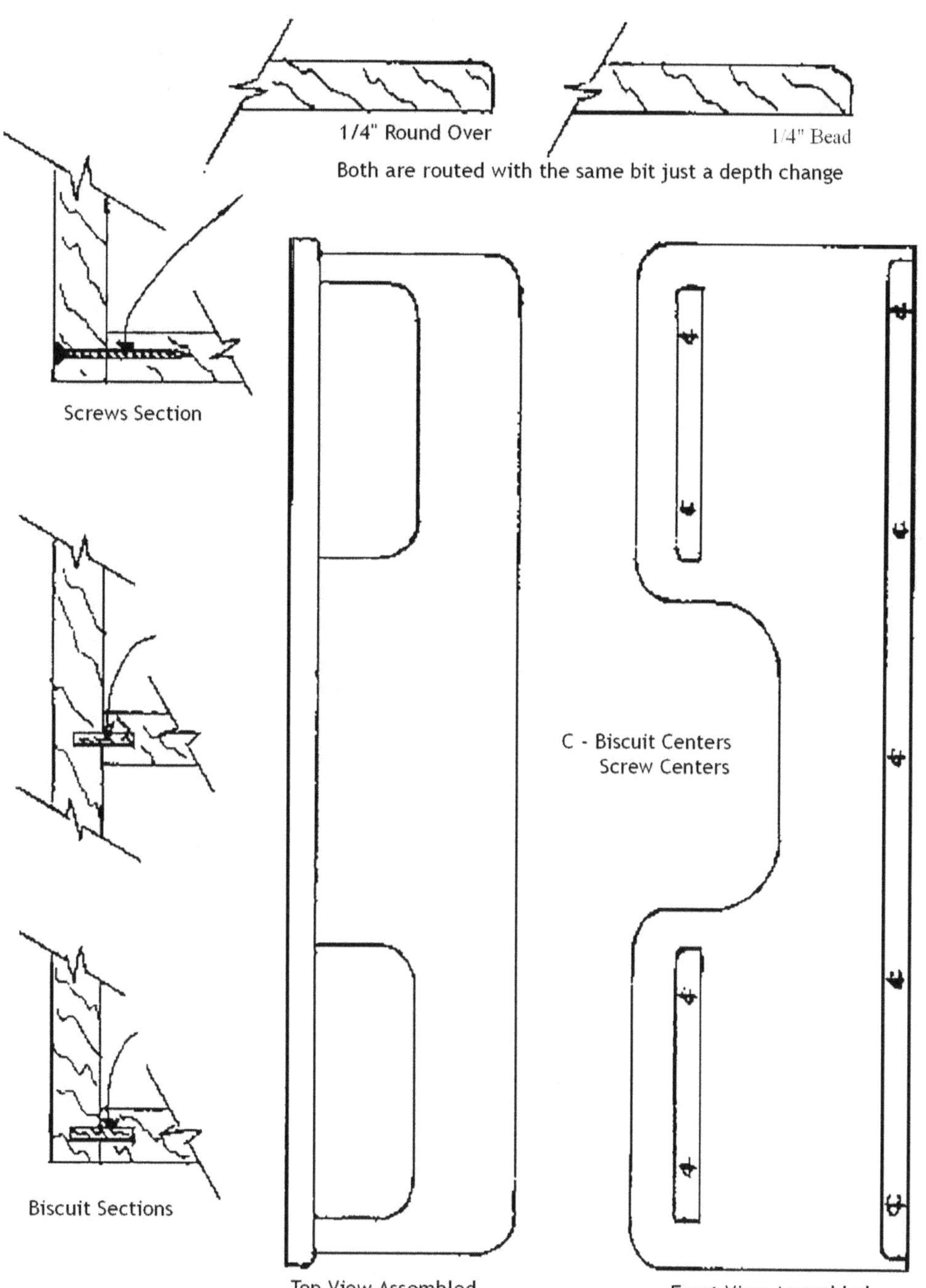
1/4" Round Over
1/4" Bead
Both are routed with the same bit just a depth change
Screws Section
Biscuit Sections
C - Biscuit Centers
Screw Centers
Top View Assembled
Front View Assembled

Notes

PROJECT FOUR: CHILD'S TABLE

Child's Table Instructions

Materials List: For this project I suggest white pine that is readily available. You will need only 2 8 foot pieces of 1 X 6 for the entire project if you layout carefully before cutting. All the dimensions are clearly described in the drawings. Just cut the following rectangular pieces and then cut the shapes as described in the next section.

4 - 3/4" X 5" X 24"

2 - 3/4" X 3" X 18 1/2"

2 - 3/4" X 3" X 17"

4 - 3/4" X 2" X 19"

2 - 3/4" X 3/4" X 15 1/2"

Cutting the Parts: The parts for this project can be cut entirely with a table saw. Cut the pieces for the Table Top first. Cut 4 pieces of the 1 X 6 24 inches long. Rip each of these four pieces to 5 inches wide. Next cut the Aprons. To make better use of the material, cut four pieces of 1 X 6 19 inches long. Rip a 3 inch wide piece from each of the four 19 inch pieces. Cut two of the 3 inch wide pieces to 18 1/ 2 inches long and two to 17 inches long. Next rip a 2 inch wide piece from each of the left over pieces. From the last piece of 1 X 6 you have left, rip 4 pieces 5/8 inch wide. Cut two of the 5/8 inch pieces 21 inches long and two of them 15 1/ 2 inches long.

Sanding the Edges: Sand all the edges lightly with a belt sander to remove all excess roughness. Take care to keep the sander upright and moving smoothly to avoid gouging the wood. Clamp each piece tightly before sanding.

Routing the Edges: Only the edges of the Table Top pieces require routing. Select the top faces and mark the bottom face of all four Table Top pieces. Next place them edge-to-edge on your worktable checking the fit and moving pieces around for the tightest possible fit. Sand the joints that remain open more than a fraction with a belt sander to improve the fit. This step can also be done with a hand plane or a jointer. Once the fit is acceptable, flip all the pieces over and realign them face down. Then make a large V mark across the bottom face of all four pieces to make certain you will remember how they come together. When it is time to assemble the Table Top, the V must come together for the pieces to be in the correct position. Now mark an X on the top and bottom face of each edge that will be routed. Start by marking an X on all four edges of all four pieces on the top face. Now flip the four pieces over maintaining the same relationship to each piece and mark the bottom face. On the two outside pieces mark the two ends and the outside edge. On the two inside pieces mark only the two ends.

Place a 1/ 4 inch round over bit in your router and set the depth of the bit for a standard 1/ 4 inch round over as shown in the drawings. Then round over the edges that you marked with an X only. These pieces are large enough to clamp and use a handheld router. My preference with most small projects is to use a router table. It is a much safer and easier operation with a router table. Round over each piece and return it to its proper position on the worktable with the bottom face up. In this position you are prepared to mark the biscuit locations.

Biscuit Layout and Cutting: Start by laying out and cutting the biscuit slots for the Table Top. Place the four Table Top pieces on your worktable face down. Arrange them so the V mark that you previously made comes together correctly. Measure along each joint with your tape and mark across both boards at 2 inches, 7 inches, 12 inches, 17 inches and 22 inches. Do this on all three joints. Take the first piece and clamp it to the worktable face up. Clamp each piece overhanging the edge of your workbench so the biscuit slots can be cut. Set the fence of the biscuit joiner to 1/ 4 inch deep and set the depth of cut for a size 20 biscuit. Place the fence of the biscuit joiner flat on the work piece and align the guideline on the first mark. Cut the biscuit slot and repeat the same process on the one edge of the outside pieces and both edges of the inside pieces. Put the Table Top pieces aside for now and get two of the Legs and one 18 1/ 2 inch Apron and place them on the worktable. Flat on the table, arrange them in correct order. The two Legs on each side of the Apron and flush with the top edge.

Measure down the joint 1 1\2 inch and mark across the two pieces. Repeat on the other joint. Clamp the Apron on the worktable and cut the biscuit slots in the same manner as before. Now clamp down each of the Legs and cut the slots in them. Place the other two Legs and the other 18 1/ 2 inch Apron on the work table and repeat the process. Get the shorter Aprons and place them flat on the worktable. Place two of the Legs against them correctly. The correct position is on edge, against the Apron and flush with the top. To make certain that the Legs are properly oriented for this, check that the line used to cut the previous biscuit slots are on the outside surface and on the top edge of the Leg. Check this carefully or you will cut the biscuit slot incorrectly. Now measure down from the top edge of the apron 1 1/ 2 inch and mark both ends. Using a small square, carry the lines down to the outside edge of each Leg and mark the location of the biscuit on the top edge of the Leg.

Repeat this process with the other apron. Clamp these Apron pieces to the worktable and cut the biscuit slots as you did with the other Apron pieces. Now clamp the Legs upright with the outside edge facing up. Now place the fence of the biscuit joiner on the leg edge and the base against the Leg and align the biscuit joiner with the mark. Cut the biscuit slot and repeat this process on all four legs. When making these cuts always make certain that the fence of the biscuit joiner is flat on the edge of the leg and the face of the biscuit joiner is flat against the work piece. This will ensure accurate, properly aligned cuts.

Sanding: It is always easier to sand project parts prior to assembly. Use a random orbit sander or an orbital sander with 120-grit sandpaper to clean up all the imperfections on the surfaces. Do not sand off the biscuit marks or the V mark on the tabletop pieces until after you have glued them together. Also hand sand all the round overs that you routed. For the most part these round overs will be smooth enough but when you rout across the grain it tends to get rough. Sand all the rough areas to ensure a smooth finished product.

Assembly: Assembling a project using biscuits requires a little planning. If you don't plan the process you may wind up placing glue in a biscuit slot and having to turn the piece upside down allowing the glue to flow out and make a mess. The first step with the assembly of this project is to assemble the Table Top. Start by putting glue in the slots on one of the outside pieces. Remember to use the glue sparingly. Use a glue bottle tip that has a small round opening and run a thin bead of glue just inside each slot on both sides. If you have done this properly the slot will not fill up and the glue will not ooze out when you insert the biscuit. If the glue oozes out you are using too much glue. Lighten up before you continue. You can also use a small art brush to spread the glue smoothly in the slot. Make certain that the biscuits are completely inserted by tapping them with a mallet. Now take the Table Top piece that belongs next to that one and put glue in the biscuit slots. Align the board with the biscuits in the slots and tap the boards together with the mallet. Put the two pieces aside for a moment. Get the other outside piece and repeat the procedure. Now put glue in the slots of one of the pairs that are assembled and insert the biscuits. Put glue in the slots on the other pair and assemble them. Make certain the ends are aligned. Now clamp the boards together tightly.

Make certain that the boards do not curl up. Check this carefully. If the boards are curling up use clamps to take the curl out while the glue is still wet. After the top is completely flat lay it aside to dry before doing any further work to it.

To assemble the Legs and Aprons, start with the first set that was cut for biscuits. Put glue in the slots on each end of the Apron. Tap in the biscuits. Put glue in the slots on the edge of each Leg and quickly insert the biscuit in the Apron into the slots. Once the Apron is inserted into the two Legs, tap them tightly and then clamp it. Put this aside and do the other corresponding set. When assembling these Leg sets make certain that the marks you made are on the same side to assure that you are assembling correctly. Check both assemblies for squareness. Remember, this can be done with a square or by measuring the diagonal. Both diagonals must be the same or the assembly is out of square. If the assembly is out of square, the final assembled table will not sit flat on the floor.

After the glue has dried, release the clamps. Put glue into each end of the remaining Aprons and tap in biscuits. Lay one of the assembled Leg sets on the worktable with the biscuit slots facing up. Put glue in the slots and quickly insert the Apron biscuits. Make certain that you line up the marks for correct orientation. Now lay the other Leg set down on the worktable and put glue in the slots. Grab the Leg/Apron assembly and turn it over so you can insert the Apron biscuits into the other Leg set. Put the table leg structure upside down on the worktable and clamp it together. Now flip it over, right side up and make certain the top of the Legs and Aprons are flush. Correct if necessary with a mallet. Next check for squareness. If there is a problem, it can be corrected by using a clamp diagonally across on the longest diagonal. Tightening the clamp will bring the project into square. Check frequently as you tighten the clamp and stop when you have attained the correct measurement. Also check that all four legs are flat on your worktable.

Allow the glue to dry and then install the 5/8 inch X 3/ 4 inch Strips. These Strips are used to attach the Table Top to the table frame. Drill three holes through each 5/8 inch X 3/ 4 inch piece in each direction. Ream each of the screw holes slightly. Use 1 1/ 4 inch self tapping drywall screws to attach the pieces to the inside of the table frame. They should be attached to the sides with the short Aprons with the 5/8 inch side screwed and glued. Make certain the strips are flush with the top edge. The final step for assembly is to fasten the Table Top to the table frame. Start by putting the Table Top face down on the worktable. Now place the table frame upside down on the bottom of the Table Top. Center the table frame correctly over the Table Top and then insert 1 1/ 4 inch screws through the holes in the Strips and into the bottom of the Table Top. Do not use glue here. There should be at least three screws through each of the Strips. To make things easier, leave the Table Top off until you have completed the finish.

Finishing: Sand the entire project lightly with 220-grit sandpaper either by hand or with an orbital sander. This is a very light sanding since you already sanded all the surfaces before assembly. If you want a darker color than the natural wood, apply a stain of your choice.

Follow the instructions on the stain can but remember that stains must be wiped thoroughly to remove all streaks. Allow the stain to dry overnight and then apply 2 or 3 coats of varnish, polyurethane or Deft. Sand by hand with 400-grit sandpaper between coats to ensure a very smooth final finish. I suggest you use a satin or semi-gloss clear finish for a smooth rich furniture look.

Table Top Option: For a Table Top without the grooves, much more work is involved. You must glue up the boards edge to edge. For this option, do not router the top and bottom edges of the Table Top pieces prior to assembly. You can follow the same board selection procedure and mark the boards with the V as you would for the grooved job. You will also use the biscuits in the same manner, however, for this option the biscuits will only serve to align the boards to reduce the amount of final sanding.

Start by placing the first set of biscuits as before. This time instead of just placing glue in the second slots, spread the glue over the entire edge of the board. Put the first two boards together and then the second two boards in the same way. Now glue up the two sets in the center and your Table Top is ready for clamping. Clamp the pieces together snugly and align the ends with a mallet. Now tighten the clamps. To ensure that the Table Top remains flat, place clamps on both the bottom and top side of the Table Top. When you glue up boards like this, a lot of glue will ooze out. I suggest that you use newspaper over your bench before starting this job. Don't try to wipe the excess glue off the joints while it is wet. Allow the glue to set up for about thirty minutes then clean off the excess easily with a putty knife. Remove as much glue as possible because it will impede sanding when it dries. Wait overnight before removing the clamps. After the glue is dry, remove all the clamps. Use a paint scraper to remove any excess glue that remained. Use a belt sander with 100-grit sanding belts to sand both the top and bottom surfaces until the glue joints are clean and smooth. Always sand with the grain, not against it. The joints should be almost invisible.

When sanding with a belt sander it is essential to keep the sander moving. Move forward, backward and side-to-side but keep moving. Do not apply pressure down on the sander. Let the weight of the machine do the work even if it takes quite a while to clean up the joints. If you apply pressure the surface could easily be gouged and the sander will be overheated. Plus, the excess friction may damage the belt. If you allow the sander to work with its own weight it will remain upright and not gouge the surface.

After sanding the faces, sand all the edges. Then sand the faces again with your random orbit or finishing sander to remove any scratches that the belt sander may have caused. Finally, rout the top and bottom edges and install the Table Top on the legs as previously described.

CHILD'S TABLE DRAWINGS

Drawings are not to scale. Use listed dimensions

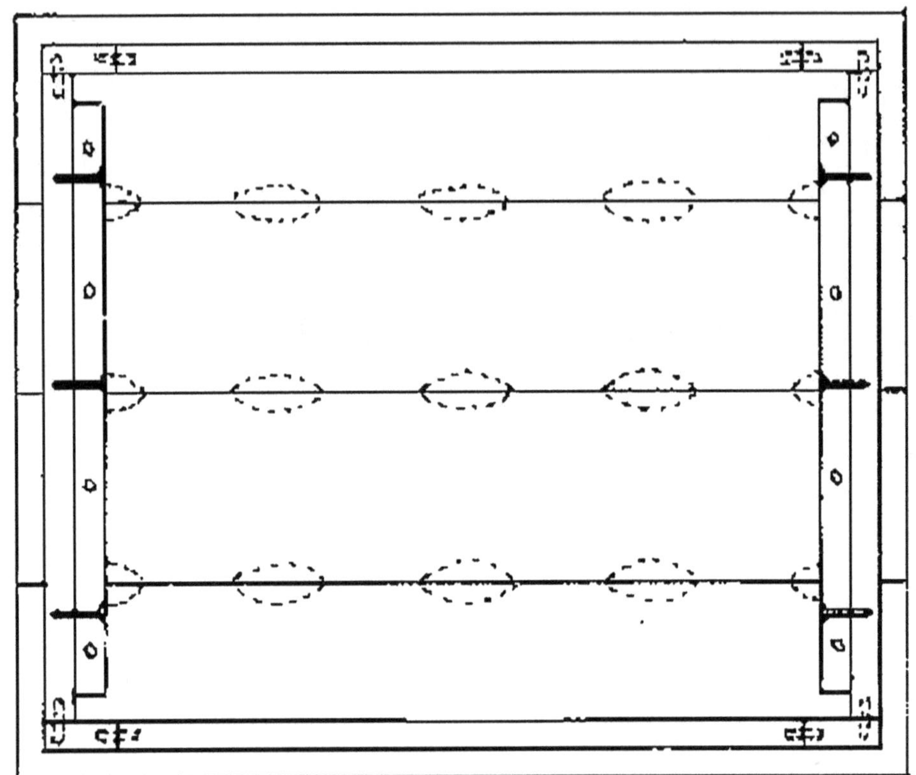

Bottom View Assembled

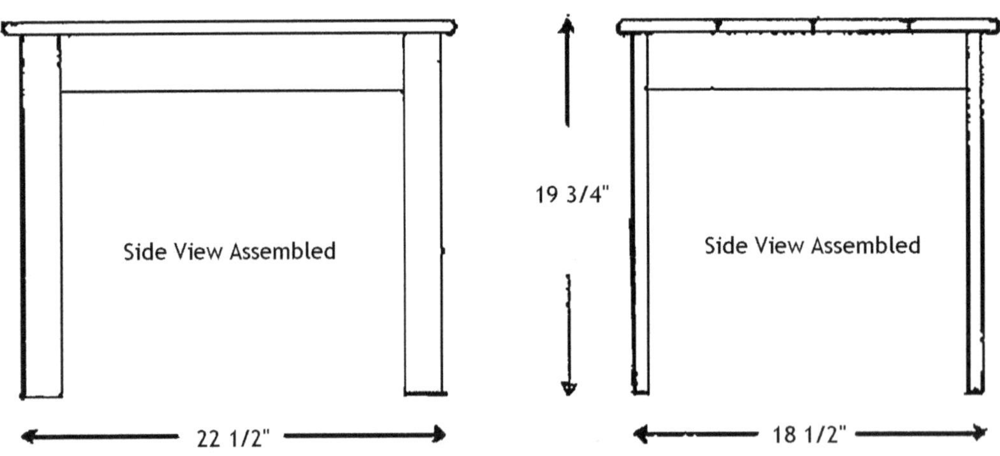

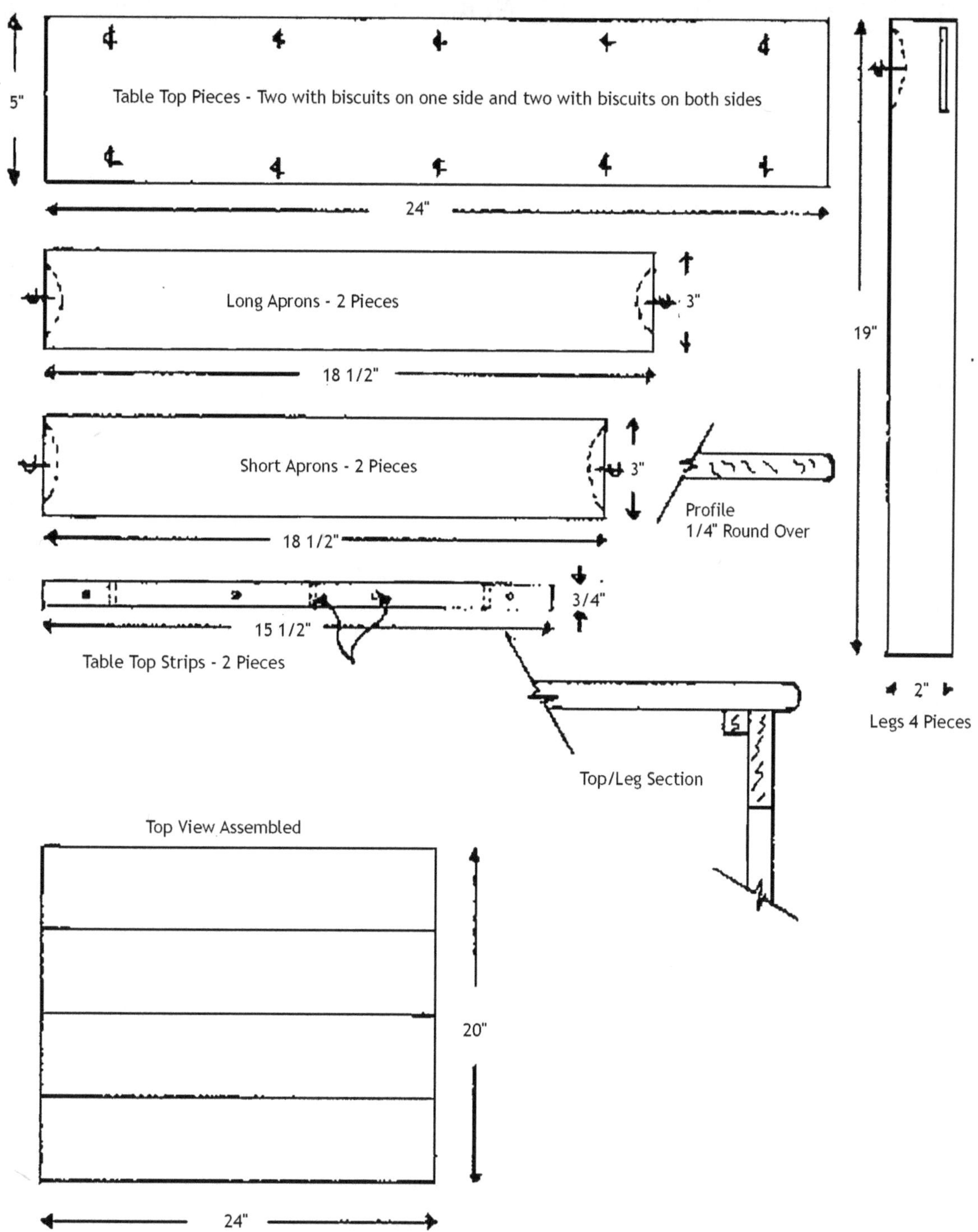

5"
Table Top Pieces - Two with biscuits on one side and two with biscuits on both sides
24"
Long Aprons - 2 Pieces
3"
18 1/2"
Short Aprons - 2 Pieces
3"
18 1/2"
Profile
1/4" Round Over
3/4"
15 1/2"
Table Top Strips - 2 Pieces
Top/Leg Section
19"
2"
Legs 4 Pieces
Top View Assembled
20"
24"

Notes

PROJECTS MADE USING BISCUIT JOINERY

The next few pages contain photos of projects I built using biscuit joinery. In some projects it was used more than others but all of them take advantage of the simpler joinery methods of the Biscuit Joiner.

It would be difficult for me to come up with an accurate count of the hundreds of cabinets and furniture pieces that I built over my almost thirty years as a full-time woodworking professional. The Biscuit Joiner played a huge role in most of those projects both large and small. While I accumulated photos of some of those projects, some of which appear on my web sites and blogs, I decided to limit the photos in this book to projects that I built for our home since leaving the woodworking profession.

The projects pictured in this section were built in a small personal shop using many consumer model tools, including the Ryobi Biscuit Joiner used for most of the projects. Without exception, all of the projects shown in the photos that follow can be seen in my home.

Let's start with two simple, decorative shelves. The first is in a bedroom converted to an office in our home and it is a long, narrow, wall mounted shelf where we display various family photos.

This shelf is basically just one piece of white pine 1X6 with two shelf supports biscuit jointed with a T joint into the top shelf. Then the two shelf supports are screwed to the wall either into a stud or anchors.

The other simple, decorative shelf below is in the sun room at the rear of our home and serves to hold a small leaf lamp. This shelf is three pieces of white pine with round over edges and biscuit jointed together and screwed to the wall.

The next three photos shown on the next two pages are of the complete kitchen I built in our home. After the third photo on the next page there is some information about this kitchen and the use of the Biscuit Joiner.

This kitchen replaced the old one that was the original contractor grade kitchen in the home. After a small flood the particle board base cabinets were ruined so I finally decided to build a complete new kitchen. The doors were built using biscuits in square frame joints throughout.

Notice the special design features on the cabinet above and the others. Above I created an open section for the radio and some decorative pieces and I had an electrician put in an outlet so the wires wouldn't hang down under the cabinet. On the other upper cabinets I built in a bookcase for recipe books and a place for a small microwave oven.

In addition to those features the cabinets have pull out shelves throughout and every shelf and drawer has drawer slides that pull out 1 inch beyond full extension.

This is an interesting cabinet in our living room. We have a wall mounted TV in our bedroom but when the kids came to visit they complained about no TV in the living room. We didn't want a TV visible all the time in the living room so I built this cabinet that houses a 32 inch flat screen TV. The two doors that were assembled using square biscuit frame joints open to reveal the TV which pulls out of the cabinet and swivels.

Notice that the cabinet is in a corner and runs almost to another corner. I could not have made it any larger so there was no room for doors that recess into the cabinet. Notice also that the hinges on the door are visible in black. It was my intent to use European concealed hinges but I had to use the bulky 180 degree hinges so the doors would open wide enough. Once the cabinet was completed everything worked perfectly except that the TV could not be pulled out of the cabinet because it was blocked by the large hinges.

I resolved the problem by removing the European hinges and replaced them with small black butt hinges that worked well.

This is the coffee table in our living room which is assembled almost entirely with biscuit joinery. It is built of white pine with a nice stain that fits well with the solid teak flooring.

The four legs are basically corner joints and after all four were glued up they were biscuit jointed to the table apron using an edge-to-edge biscuit joint. Notice the round over detail on all parts of the table. This was done by rounding over the pieces with a router and a round over carbide-tipped bit. It's important to remember that the legs are biscuit jointed to the apron by using glue only on the biscuit joints. Since both the edge of the table apron and the edge of the table legs are rounded over you can't apply glue to the joint itself. This poses no problem since the joints are sufficiently strong with just the biscuits being glued.

The tabletop is now tile but originally it was plastic laminate with a decorative wood edge that was biscuit jointed to the edge . Once the table was completed my wife did not like the look of the plastic laminate so I made a wood riser around the top of the table the thickness of tile and then we glued tile on the table within the wood border.

The table top is fastened to the legs and apron with 3/4 inch X 3/ 4 inch blocks along the inside of the apron. These are glued to the inside of the apron and then screwed to the bottom of the tabletop.

This is an end table in our living room made to match the coffee table on the previous page except that it has a drawer for storage. Notice that the drawer is designed to match the table apron on the other three sides. The tabletop is edged and tiled exactly like the coffee table.

This is what I call an end table/desk. It is still in our bedroom and was originally built to place next to our bed where the wider part on the left side would serve as the end table and the rest of it could be used as a desk for writing.

Notice the half round edge on the countertop which is covered with plastic laminate. This edge and the custom stain color was created to match the headboard we had at the time it was built. We no longer have that headboard and this end table/desk is now relegated to serve as storage and a place for family photos.

The two boxes are biscuit jointed plywood. The two drawers and two doors come in handy for storage of many things.

This is an interesting little project. It is a dual level table serving a dual purpose. It is out in the sun room and the top is used for decorative items and the bottom for magazines which were removed for this photo to reveal the details of the table.

This project was another one built during my power tool demonstrations for the Skil Power Tool company at Home Depot stores. The tops and the aprons are made of white pine boards and the legs were cut from white pine 2X4s. The legs and aprons were rounded over with a 1/ 4 inch round over router bit.

The corners of the top and bottom levels were cut out to clear the legs and provide an extra detail. This entire table was completed during one demonstration in a tiny shop space in the store.

The projects on the next three pages are in the bedroom that we converted to an office for both of us. I have one corner of the office for my writing and my wife has the other corner for her writing.

The storage cabinet above has nine storage drawers of various depths and two file drawers on the right hand side. The entire project is made of maple plywood with a solid plywood edge biscuit jointed to the top.

The drawers are made of 1/ 2 inch maple plywood with 1/ 4 inch plywood bottoms. The cabinet serves to store all our office supplies and other small items.

The top is a good work surface but also serves for decorative items, plants, and a lamp. Notice that the decorative shelf included in a previous page is located directly above this cabinet.

This straight forward bookcase is located in the office directly above my wife's desk. The bookcase was built with white pine 1X10 lumber and assembled with basic biscuit joinery. After assembly the front edge of all the boards was rounded over using a 1/ 4 inch round over bit on a router.

The bookcase has no back but it does have a cleat at the rear top of the bookcase to facilitate screwing the bookcase to the wall. After finding the location of the studs I used screws to hold the bookcase in place.

The shelf across the top is just a 1X12 inch piece that goes around two of the walls in the office and holds decorative items.

This photo shows a small section on my workstation. This is a simple desk plan. The drawer unit has two regular drawers and one file drawer.

The entire desk was built of paint grade birch plywood and finished only with a clear coat.

The drawer fronts extend beyond both sides of the cabinet by 1/ 2 inch and then they are rounded over and this forms the handles to open the drawers. It is a simple and inexpensive design that serves me well.

The top is also paint grade birch plywood well sanded with several coats of clear wood finish.

This is a simple cedar chest plan that is completely assembled using biscuit joinery. The case is made entirely of oak plywood that originally had a light stain and clear coat. My wife later gave it this finish to make it more colorful.

The chest has a lid at the top that in this case is covered by a removable custom made cushion and two small pillows. At the bottom there is a drawer. The floor of the chest between the top of the drawer and the bottom of the top chest space is made of cedar installed so it serves both the top chest space and the drawer. Right now we keep toys in it for when our grandchildren visit.

This photo and the one on the previous page are of the china cabinet shown on the dining set on the cover. This cabinet is unusual in that it was built around the stained glass door inserts. The stained glass was a wedding present that we hung in our bedroom windows for years. When we decided to build a new dining room set with a china cabinet my wife came up with the idea of using the stained glass inserts for the doors of the china cabinet.

To make certain the doors would fit the cabinet after I designed it, I built the doors to fit the stained glass first and then built the china cabinet to fit the doors. The doors and the side panels are assembled with biscuit joinery.

To match the carving on the dining table, the counter top, drawer fronts, front edge, and the top apron are all carved just like the table. The rest of the cabinet is maple plywood and solid maple with a stain and clear coat.

The photo on the previous page is a corner cabinet that I built for our hallway. The design was my wife's idea. She knew exactly what she wanted including the finish which she applied herself. The flower design on the top apron is simply a hole drilled through with petals carved into the wood to form a flower design. Like many of the pieces in our home it was made with paint grade birch plywood and white pine lumber for the face frames.

The cabinet above is the most recent addition to our home. I built it for our master bathroom when we remodeled it completely. The door and drawer frames were made of clear grade pine and the door and drawer panels were made of 1/ 2 inch birch plywood with grooves cut with a router to give the impression of planks.

The drawer fronts were first made as doors and then cut down for drawer fronts so the design would match the doors. The countertop is plywood with a solid piece biscuit jointed to the front edge. Then the top and front edge were covered with plastic laminate. Finally, I used a router with a 1/ 4 inch cove bit to cut through the laminate and form the front edge which I then finished with stain and several coats of spar varnish.

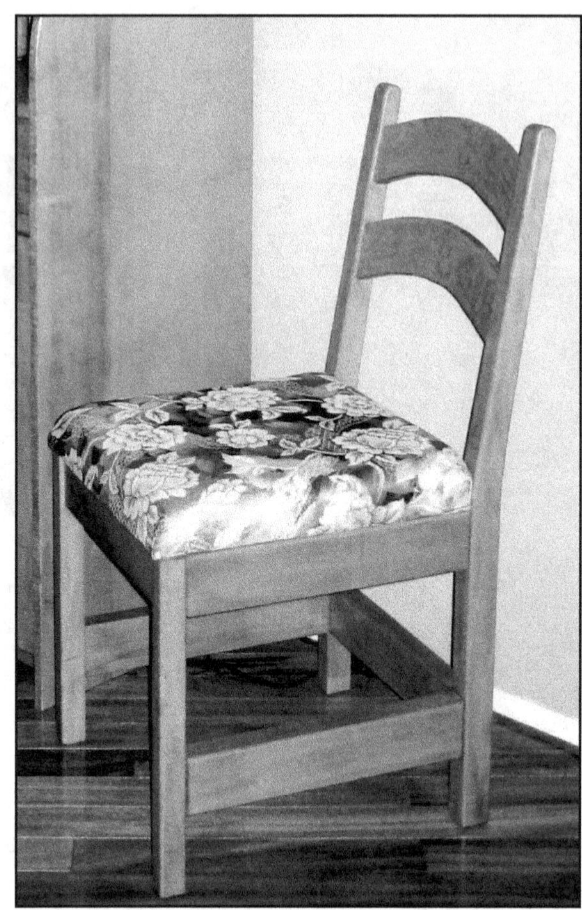

My entire dining room set is based on a Southwest design and that includes the chairs. Except for the cushion, the chair is made entirely of 8/4 solid maple that I planed to 1 3/ 4 inch thickness.

With the exception of the back pieces, every single joint has three biscuits spaced within each joint. I used the Biscuit Joiner without the fence and with spacers to cut all the biscuit slots.

All of the pieces were rounded over using a 1/ 4 inch round over router bit and that gave a nice accent to all the joints. I prefer that design to just gluing up and then sanding the joints smooth because it adds an interesting accent to the design. Someone else may prefer the smooth unaccented joint. It could have been done either way.

I assembled and glued up the two sides first but could not assemble the sides to each other until I had completed the back pieces which had to be cut to shape and then carved to match the table.

The backs were the most difficult part of the chair. They were cut from a piece of 1 3/ 4 X 6 inch maple stock. To make them I first cut this stock to the correct size to fit between the sides. Next I determined exactly where I needed to make the biscuit slot cut and cut one slot on each side.

The next step was to draw the top shape of the back piece so that the cut did not expose the biscuit slot. Next, I used a large band saw to cut the top shape of the back pieces. Once that was done, I put the pieces with the loose biscuits back in place and drew the shape of the front of the back pieces again making certain that I stayed clear of the biscuit slots.

Once again I cut the shapes out carefully using the band saw. After cutting the top and front shapes, the back pieces were complete except for the carving. I then clamped the pieces and carefully carved the front, back, top, and bottom of every back piece to match the tabletop.

Finally, after all of this was done I could use the two back pieces together with the three cross structure pieces to biscuit joint the chair together.

This entire dining room set was completed many years ago and always draws complements from visitors.

Notes

BISCUIT JOINERY DRAWINGS

The next few pages contain simple drawings of various joints that can be done with a Biscuit Joiner with details of how each joint can be used and how they relate to the project plans in this book. Over the years I have used the Biscuit Joiner to make these joints for projects for myself and for customers. You can use these joints to assemble your own projects taking full advantage of the Biscuit Joiner.

I sincerely believe that using biscuit joinery can help you make excellent projects with strong yet easy to do joints whether you are a home woodworker or a part-time or full-time professional.

I hope that the joints described in these pages serve to interest you in biscuit joinery and lead to the creation of even more joints that can be made with the Biscuit Joiner.

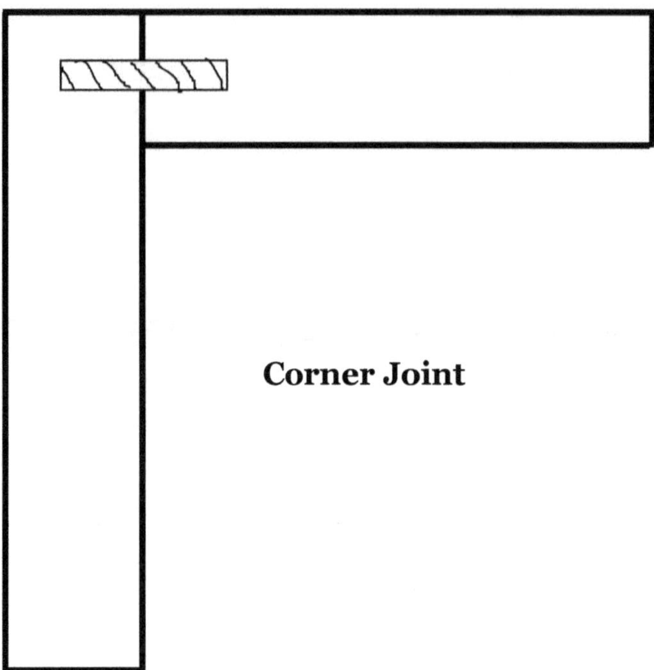

Corner Joint

The corner joint is basically a butt joint which involves the edge or end of one board and the face of another. These joints can be simply the width of one board or the length of an entire sheet of plywood or MDF fiberboard.

The number of biscuits used on these joints is based on that width or length. On a 1X4 board only 1 size 20 biscuit will fit. On a 1X6 board you can fit 2 size 20 biscuits.

When doing joints like this it's important to remember that glue works best on long grain. That is the grain that runs along the length of a board whether on the edge or the face. The wood at the ends of a board, and at any location where you create an end by cutting the board, are called end grain. While you can use biscuits to attach an end grain to a long grain, it is not a good idea to join two end grain pieces even with good joinery. For the best possible joinery glue together pieces using the long grain whenever possible.

The end grain/long grain issue does not apply to plywood since the direction of the grain in the various layers is different.

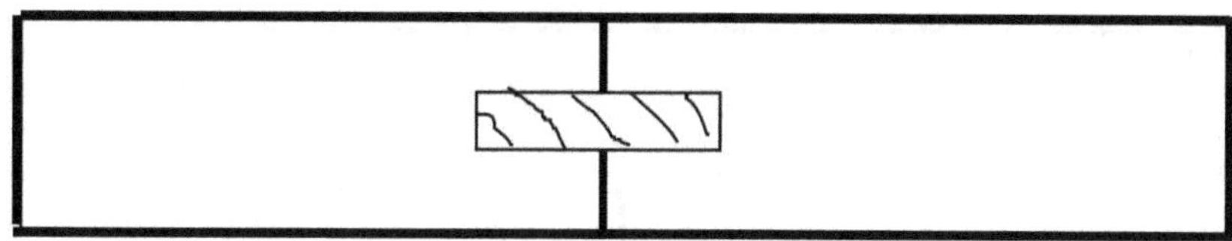

Edge to Edge Joint

This is a joint that is often misused because of a lack of understanding about gluing up boards. When gluing up boards edge-to-edge in order to create wider boards, it's important to remember that in this kind of joint the biscuits serve only to maintain the alignment of the boards while the glue is drying.

The biscuits may add strength but it's unnecessary on this kind of joint. That's because the glue joint, once dry, is stronger than the wood. So, if you didn't use the biscuits the joints would be stronger than the wood itself.

If you don't believe that, conduct a simple test to prove it to yourself. Just cut a half dozen pieces of 1X4 or 1X6 6 inches long and then glue them side to side without any biscuits. Once the glue is dry, take the glued up piece and put it against something at an angle and break it with your foot or a hammer. Then take the two pieces and break them also. None of the breaks will be on the glue line. The board will always break in the wood itself. So, if the glue joint is as strong or stronger than the wood, why do you need the biscuit.

What the biscuit does is keep the boards aligned with each other easily during the glue up. Normally, boards will slip and slide because of the wetness of the glue but not with the biscuits in place. So just use sufficient biscuits to keep the two edges lined up with each other to help alignment and thereby reduce the need for so much planing or sanding to make the boards even.

When doing your glue ups remember a couple of important things. First, use lots of clamps so you maintain a tight joint throughout. Secondly, make certain the clamped pieces are straight and even with each other because you won't be able to correct that after the glue has dried. This is best done by placing clamps on the top and bottom of the glue up. Finally, clean off as much of the glue ooze as possible. I have found that the easiest way to do this is to let the glue set for 15 to 30 minutes and then use a sharp putty knife to remove the partially dried glue. This will avoid a lot of sanding later.

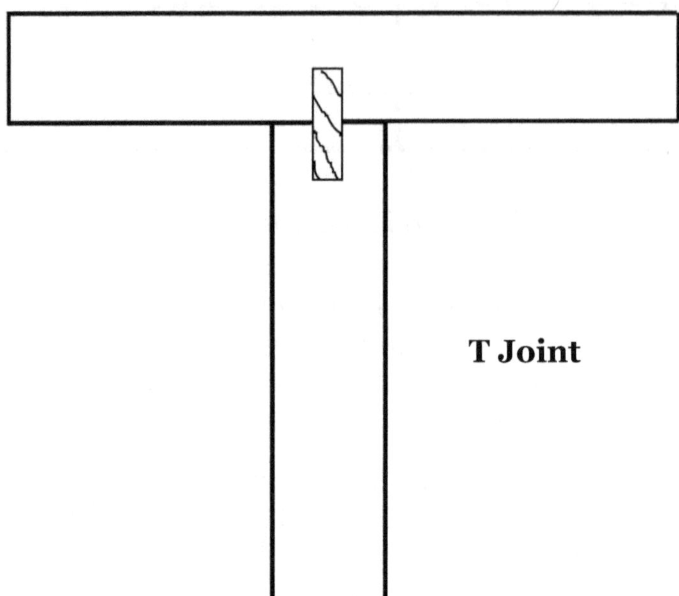

T Joint

The T Joint can be used in many ways. I use it most often to assemble cabinets made of plywood or fiberboard. This joint can be used regardless of the length of the two pieces.

You could biscuit joint two full length plywood pieces or any other length by simply spacing the biscuits appropriately depending on the strength needed for the specific project. Usually you can place the biscuits with spacing somewhere between 6 inches and 12 inches. My suggestion is to opt for the closer placement. I believe that you can never make things too strong.

The T Joint can also be used on a much smaller scale to create dividers in a cabinet or drawer. Or, to create a knick knack shelf unit with shelves at various levels and dividers. They can also be used for removable shelves or dividers by gluing biscuits into the sides of cabinets, cases, or drawers and then cutting slot into the edges of the dividers. Then the dividers can be slid over the biscuits when needed and removed when no longer needed. The dividers or shelves will remain in place. If it seems that the dividers are too loose on the biscuits, apply a very small amount of glue to the biscuits and wipe it dry. This will slightly swell the biscuit and tighten the fit.

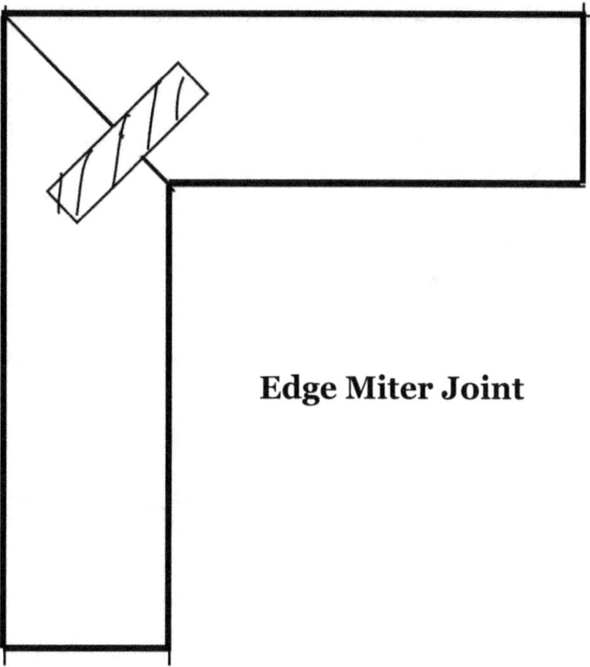

Edge Miter Joint

Edge miter joints come in handy to assemble pieces of all lengths. You can use it to make small boxes or cabinets where it is important to hide end grain. The number of biscuits used is directly related to the length of the joint. I suggest that you use a biscuit every 6 inches for most joints.

To ensure a tight joint it's important to cut the miter carefully and then cut the biscuit slots with the Biscuit Joiner properly aligned. Failure in any of these steps can lead to joints that fit badly and are weak and unattractive requiring a great deal of filler and sanding. Taking a little extra time to produce accurate pieces ensures tight accurate joints.

There are various ways to cut the biscuit slots for edge miter joints. These are covered in detail in the next section on using the Biscuit Joiner. For cutting these slots you can set the fence on your Biscuit Joiner to 45 degrees or 135 degrees if that setting is available on your Biscuit Joiner. My preference for this cut is to leave my Biscuit Joiner fence set at 90 degrees and clamp the two mitered pieces back-to-back to form a 90 degree corner. That accommodates my Biscuit Joiner with the 90 degree fence setting and gives me a more stable work surface for the cut.

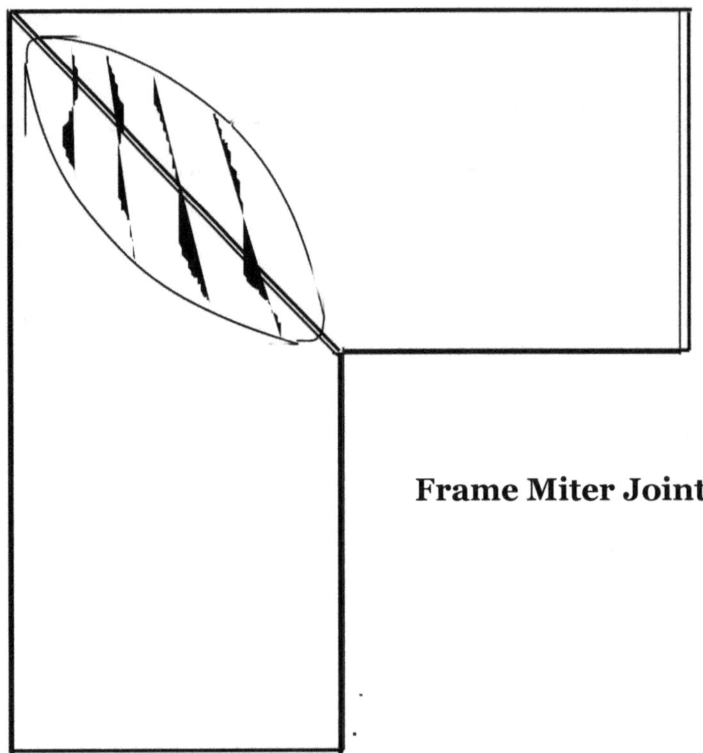

Frame Miter Joint

The frame miter joint is used mostly for frames but you can also use it to make door frames. It is a strong joint for many uses. The size of the biscuit for each application is based entirely on the size of the frame. For smaller frames you may have to use a size 0 biscuit and for larger frames you may have to use several size 20 biscuits. The important thing is to use enough biscuits to ensure a strong joint.

I prefer to cut the biscuit slots for frame miter joints using the Biscuit Joiner without the fence but you can also make the cuts using the fence. For materials thicker than 3/ 4 inch you can use a second biscuit. I would cut the slot for a second biscuit by using a spacer for the second cut but you can adjust the fence. Some users are more comfortable with the fence and accuracy can be maintained with either method.

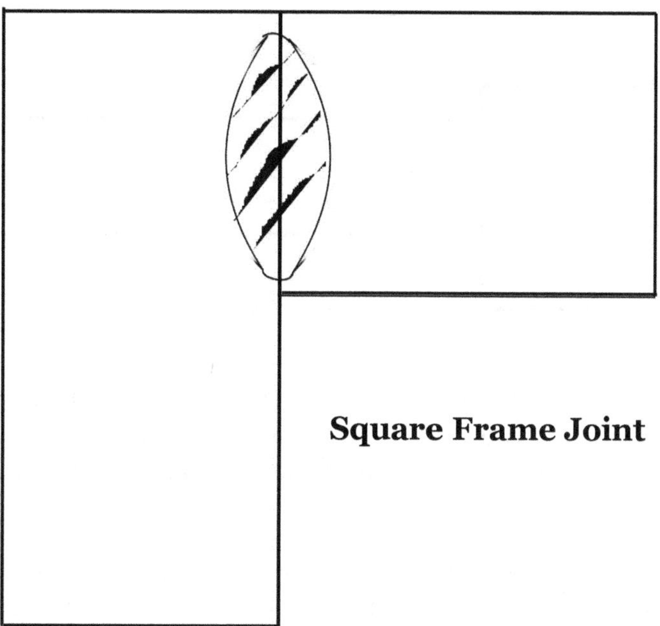

Square Frame Joint

I use the square frame joint to make doors for cabinets and furniture. All the doors for the projects in this book were made using the square frame joint cut with my Biscuit Joiner. It is a strong joint that I have used for many years on hundreds of projects.

I always cut the biscuit slots for this joint using the Biscuit Joiner without the fence. By clamping each piece to the work table and then guiding the cut with the base of the Biscuit Joiner on the work table. The blade of the Biscuit Joiner is set perfectly so when the base is on the work table the cut is centered in a 3/ 4 inch thick board.

The exact same procedure works with thicker materials simply by using spacers between the base of the Biscuit Joiner and the work table surface. For 1 inch to 1 1/ 4 inch thick material I would use a spacer for a second biscuit. For 1 3/ 4 inch thick material I would use two spacers of varying thickness and use three biscuits in the joints. This give you an extremely strong joint by creating six glue surfaces for each piece of the joint.

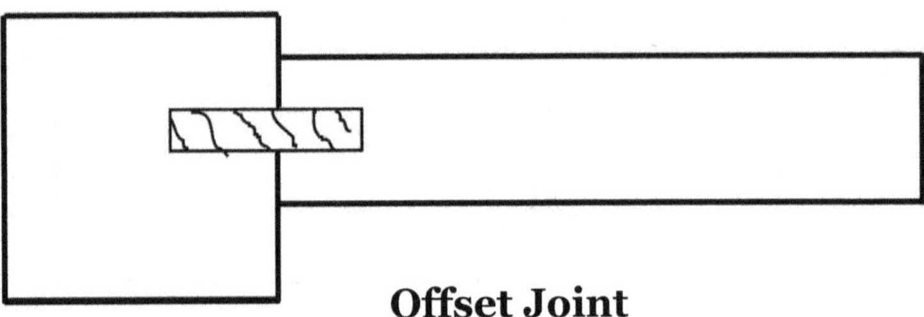

Offset Joint

The offset joint is useful to add solid wood pieces to the edges of plywood or fiberboard sheets. The number of biscuits used along this joint is determined by the strength that is needed for the particular cabinet or furniture piece.

This joint can also be used to form a strong corner for a cabinet or furniture piece. By applying a second plywood or fiberboard piece in the same manner you can form a 90 degree corner that is decorative and protects the sheet goods from damage. To make it more attractive you can round over all the corner pieces.

Years ago I was commissioned by a hotel to create a rugged design for their lecterns because they were always handled roughly. They wanted the lecterns to be made of oak plywood instead of veneered fiberboard and they wanted it to have strong corners that could be easily refinished if damaged.

I came up with a design using 3/ 4 inch thick oak plywood for the basic box with 1 3/ 4 inch X 1 3/ 4 inch corner pieces rounded over with a 1/ 4 inch round over bit. I then assembled the units with the corners extending 1/ 2 inch beyond the face of the plywood and assembled the pieces with biscuits every 6 inches throughout every joint.

The lecterns were built almost 20 years ago and are still holding up well. The corners have been sanded and refinished on some of the units because they have been run into walls or corners in the hallways but the plywood surfaces remain in good shape because they are protected by the extending corners.

In this case the offset joint served a dual purpose because it added a decorative feature to the lectern and protected the plywood veneer from normal damage.

The preceding drawings are just basic joints that can be created with the Biscuit Joiner. It is certainly not every possible joint which can possibly be created with this tool. If you are going to bond two pieces of wood to each other in some manner, chances are that biscuit joinery can be used to reinforce that joint.

Anytime you are designing a project consider the possibilities of joints made with a Biscuit Joiner. Even if you have project plans that include details on a different kind of joinery, why not consider using the Biscuit Joiner instead.

Whether the power tool is a table saw, circular saw, jig saw, scroll saw, router, sander, planer, or Biscuit Joiner, it's been my experience that we often fail to explore the full potential of a tool. Making full use of the Biscuit Joiner will help you to create projects with strong joints while still saving time. For the home woodworker that means quality projects completed faster. For the professional woodworker it means that and the potential for increased profit.

Notes

SIMPLE BISCUIT JOINERY METHODS

The next few pages contain photos of Biscuit Joiners being used for making various biscuit slots for several different joints. These are the most common methods I use now and have used for years to build projects of all sizes for myself and for customers.

The Biscuit Joiner is truly a unique tool to facilitate strong joinery in the easiest possible way. These are just a few methods and there may be many other ways that you can take advantage of the potential of Biscuit Joiners to assist you in building your own projects.

All of the illustrations that follow are of the Ryobi Biscuit Joiner. I used it for the photos because I have used it successfully for years and it is available at home improvement stores for about $100.00. It is a solid piece of equipment with some excellent features. Probably one of the most important is a fence that is easily adjustable and can be folded out of the way without removing screws or bolts.

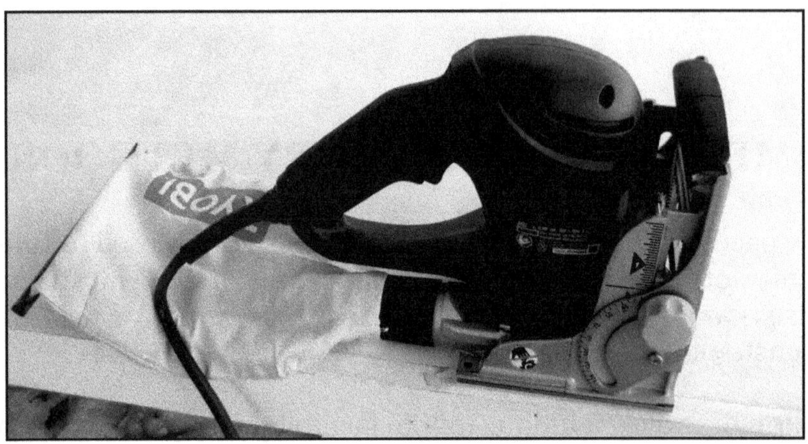

The photo above shows the Biscuit Joiner with the fence in the recessed or folded up position. This is my favorite way to use the Biscuit Joiner and the way I use it for most joinery cuts.

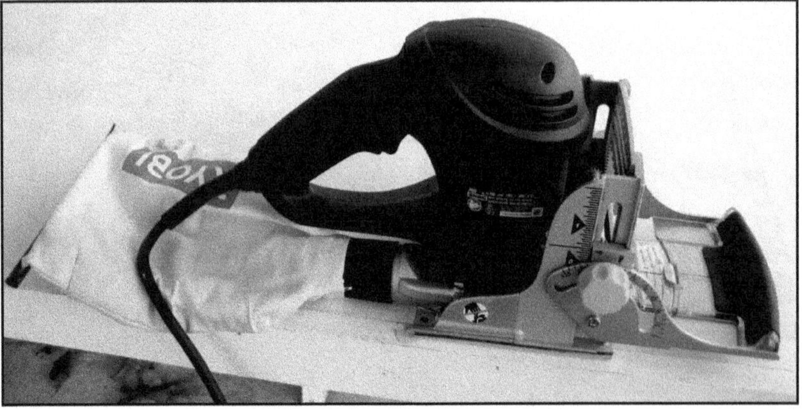

This photo shows the Biscuit Joiner with the fence ready to use at the 90 degree setting and ready for any necessary depth adjustments.

Making biscuit slots on the edge of any material using the Biscuit Joiner without the fence can serve various purposes in joinery. It can be used for edge-to-edge glue up which will be covered in more detail later in this section. It can serve to make the biscuit slots for mitered or square frames. It can be used for corner joints as shown in the range shelf project. Or, it can be used for T joints to assemble entire cabinets or to assemble bookcases like the one in this book. No matter which of these joints you are cutting, the methods are the same as shown in the next few photos even though they are more geared to the bookcase application.

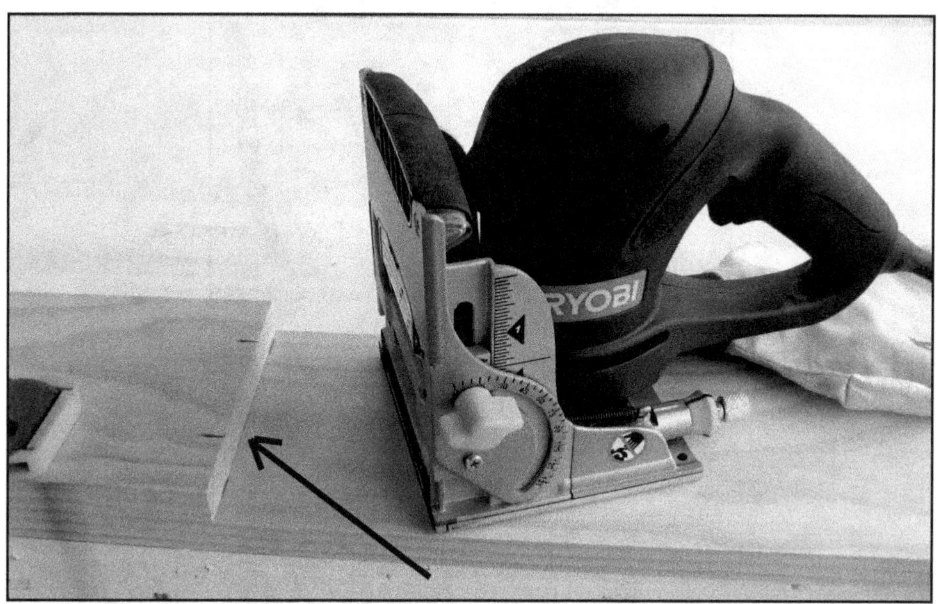

The arrow in the photo above points to the cut marks on the edge of the bookcase shelf. In most cases it's important to make these marks far enough from the edge of the board to avoid the biscuit cut going beyond the edge.

For this application I used the #20 biscuit which is 2 3/8 inches long. I placed my marks 1 3/8 inch from the edge. This allows a little extra room at the edge to make certain the cut doesn't protrude.

While protrusion of the biscuit cut may seem like a serious problem, there may be times, especially on projects that will be painted, where protrusion won't be a problem because the biscuit protrusion can be cut off and the small holes can be easily filled.

In the next two photos you can see how to make the first cuts in the sides of the bookcase by using the shelves as the guide for both the slot cuts on the sides and on the shelf edge.

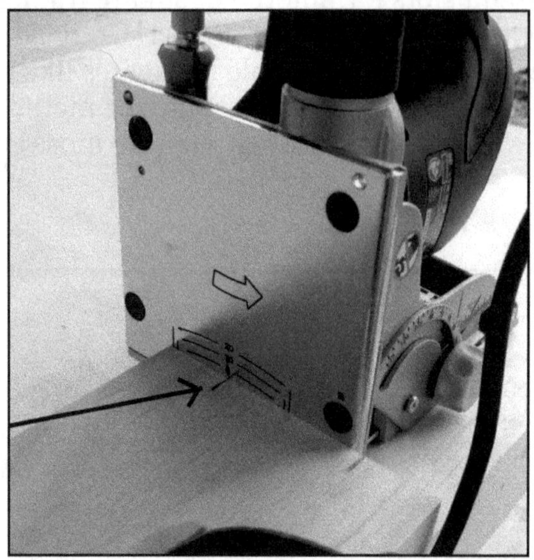

The top photo shows the position of the Biscuit Joiner upright and lined up with the slot cut mark on the edge of the shelf. This mark is used for both this slot cut and the slot cut on the edge of the shelf that is shown on the next page.

The two photos on this page show the second cuts which are made on the edge of each shelf. Since they are made using the Biscuit Joiner without the fence and placed using the same slot cut marks as the cuts on the sides, they will line up perfectly when the bookcase is assembled and it isn't necessary to mark the location of the shelves on the sides.

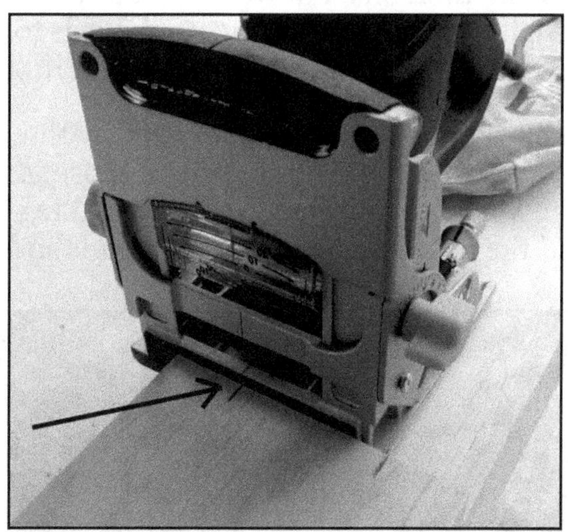

The top photo shows the Biscuit Joiner in place and ready to make the cut in the edge of the shelf. The bottom photo shows the two cuts in the edge of the shelf and the two cuts in the side of the bookcase completed.

Remember that the method described in the previous pages for using the Biscuit Joiner without a fence for the bookcase shelves and sides can be used to make the biscuit slot cuts on the edges for any joint by using any flat work surface. Just assume that the side of the bookcase in the photos is the flat work surface and the edge of the shelf is the edge of the board where the slot cuts are needed. This same method on a flat work surface can be used on the ends of mitered and square frame pieces, the edges of boards to be glued up, and on corner joints like those used on the range shelf project in this book.

While I prefer to do most of my Biscuit Joiner work without using the fence, some cuts can't be done without the fence. One of those is the edge miter joint. The photos below show my favorite way to handle making the biscuit slots for edge miter joints and the next page shows another method.

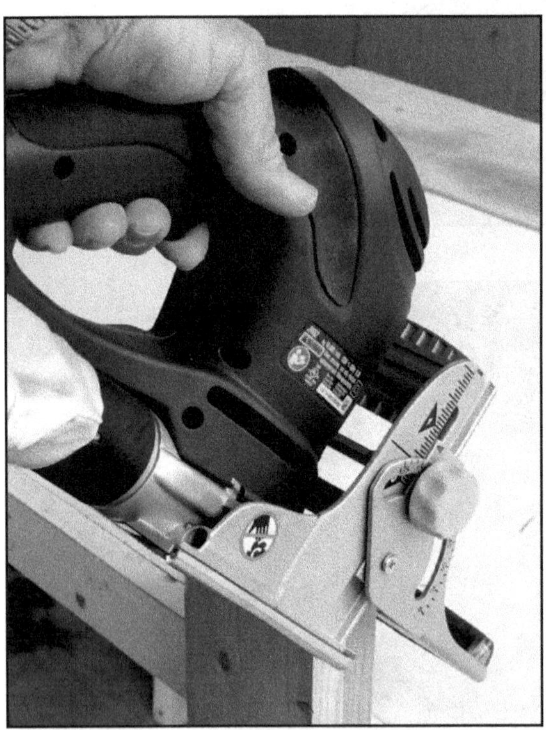

Notice that the fence is at a 90 degree angle as with a normal cut. The difference is that the depth of cut has to be adjusted to 3/ 4 inch deep instead of the normal 3/8 inch deep that it would be for a straight edge cut. This is a minor adjustment. I find this method of clamping the two pieces back to back much simpler and I believe more accurate.

Using the Ryobi or other Biscuit Joiner with a fence capable of 135 degree angle, there is another method to make the slot cuts on the mitered edge joints. The photos below show this method for which the fence is set at 135 degrees and each edge joint piece is clamped to the work table individually.

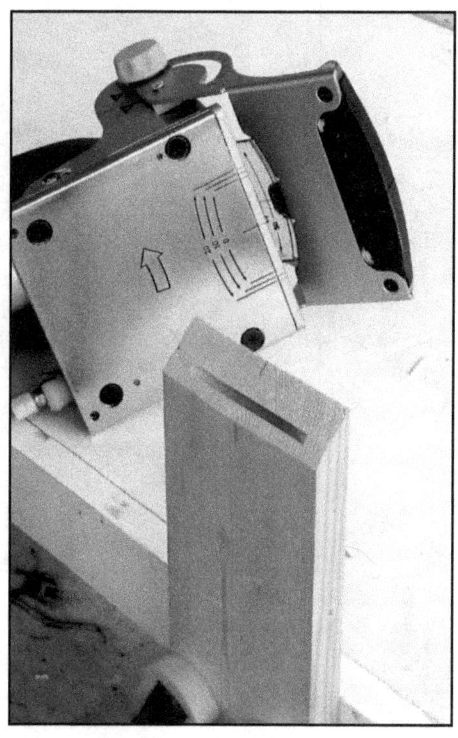

No matter the method you use for these slot cuts, make test cuts. You can set the fence correctly the first time but using a scrap piece to test the depth and location of your cuts will save you many mistakes and frustration.

Also, remember that the accuracy of these cuts is directly dependent on the placement of the Biscuit Joiner in relation to the piece you are cutting. This means viewing the placement of the Biscuit Joiner from various angles and making certain the face is against the edge fully and the fence is completely flat against the surface of the piece. If the Biscuit Joiner is not properly aligned with the work the cut will not be accurate. If one or more cuts are not accurate your piece will not assemble correctly and you may wind up doing it again. This is a waste of time and material.

Take a few minutes to make certain of the alignment and hold the Biscuit Joiner tightly when making the cuts.

Even though I prefer avoiding the fence whenever possible, the fence can be used for edge slot cuts as show below. I believe it increases the potential for misalignment but the choice is up to the user.

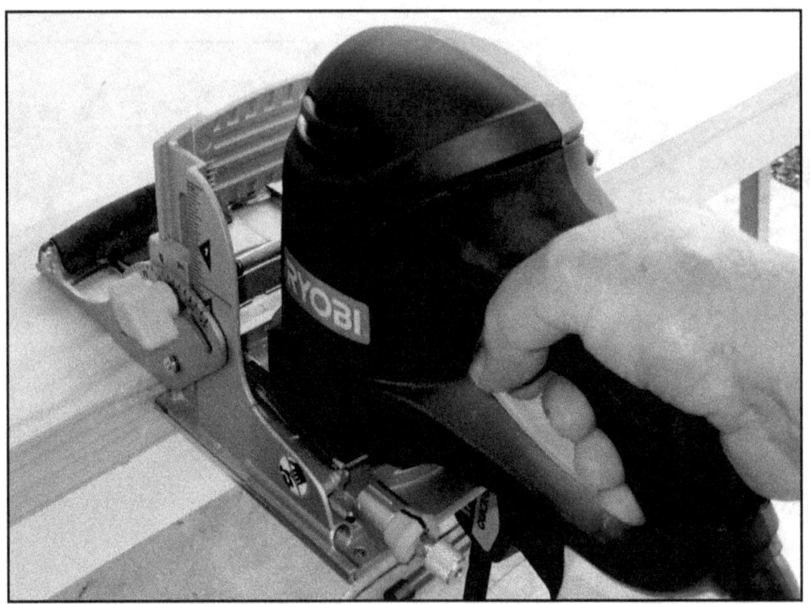

With the fence flat against the surface of the board and the face of the Biscuit Joiner flat against the edge of the board, the cut is easily made. The location of the cut can be adjusted by moving the fence up or down as needed.

At the risk of repetition, I can't overemphasize the importance of careful alignment of the the Biscuit Joiner with the work piece during the slot cuts. This also ensures the correct depth of each cut. If a cut is too shallow then the two pieces will not meet. If it is too deep then the biscuit will go further into one piece than into the other giving an uneven glue up and a weaker joint. The photos below show the method used to make certain the depth of cut is correct.

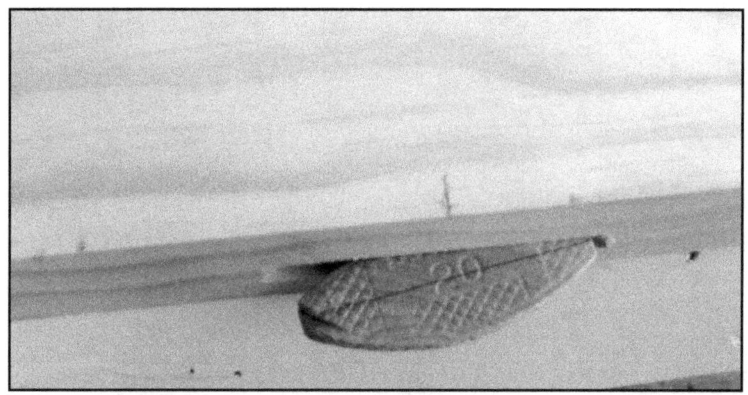

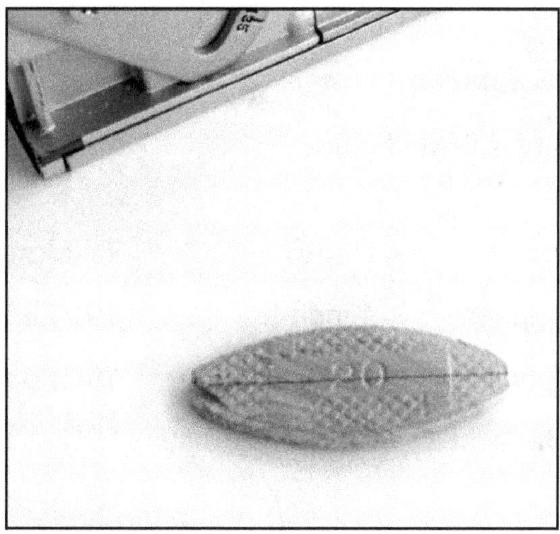

Use a sharp pencil to mark the biscuit after it is placed in the first completed slot. Then make a pencil mark across the edge and pull the biscuit out. The pencil line should be just beyond the half way mark of the biscuit. This slight difference will be offset by the glue in the slot.

There are three basic biscuit sizes including 20, 10, and 0. The three sizes are shown in the photo below.

The size of the biscuits is listed below:

Biscuit #	Length	Depth	Thickness	Inset
20	2 3/8 inches	1 inch	19/128 inch	1/ 2 inch
10	2 3/16 inches	3/ 4 inch	19/128 inch	3/8 inch
0	1 27/32 inches	5/8 inch	19/128 inch	5/16 inch

The actual size of the biscuits may vary slightly depending on the manufacturer. I have found the Porter Cable biscuits to be slightly smaller but the difference causes no issues. The depth of the slots is only slightly deeper than the inset to accommodate the glue. Thickness of the biscuits is slightly thinner than the Biscuit Joiner blade that makes a cut 5/32 inch thick and the biscuits swell with the glue to fill the difference.

In addition to preferring to avoid the fence when using the Biscuit Joiner, I also dislike the dust bags. The units I used that had dust bags all suffered from the same problem. The exhaust slot from the blade to the dust bag is too narrow and quickly becomes clogged up. For occasional use it's fine but if you will be using the Biscuit Joiner for long periods it will seem like you have to empty the bag and clean out the exhaust slot every few minutes. My solution to this problem was to use a pvc corner to divert the sawdust away from me during the cuts. This works well for me and the photo below shows the simple design on the Ryobi Biscuit Joiner.

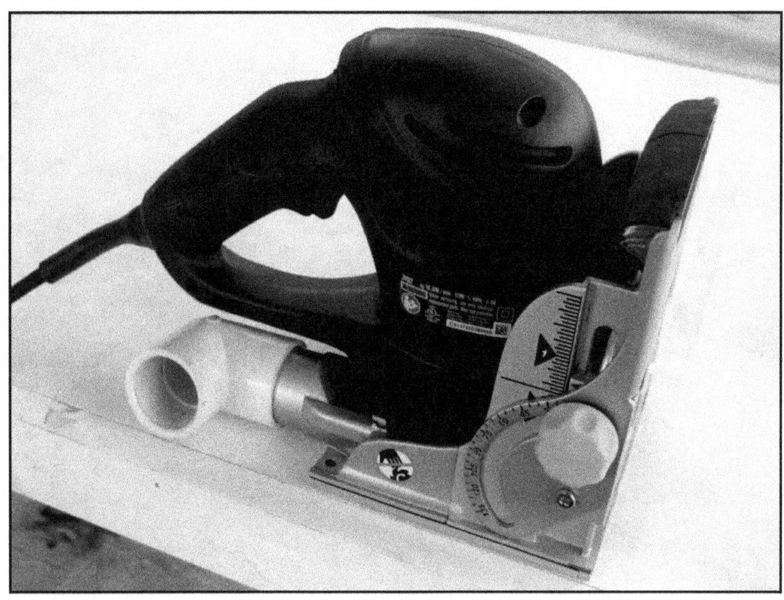

Notes

FINAL NOTES

Edge-to-Edge: Remember when gluing boards edge-to-edge the only purpose of the biscuits is to align the boards so that major planing or sanding will not be necessary after the boards are glued together. The biscuits are not necessary for the strength of the joints. When boards are glued together edge-to-edge the glue joint actually becomes stronger than the grain of the wood.

Order of Glue Up: As you check out the information in this book, especially with the projects, you will find details on the order of glue up. These may seem unimportant but following the instructions will save you from a glue mess that is difficult to clean and can lead to excessive sanding. Take a little extra time to glue things up in the best possible order and you will save time in the long run.

Slot Cut Mistakes: If you use the Biscuit Joiner regularly there will probably be some misplaced biscuit cuts. This is an easy problem to resolve by simply gluing a biscuit into the slot, let the glue dry, use a hand saw to cut the protruding part of the biscuit off, and then sand down the surface or edge and you are ready to make the cut in the correct location with just a minor delay.

Multiple Biscuit Slots or Offset Joints: If you need to have multiple slots cut for a project as I did for the chairs shown on the cover and inside this book, there is no need to use and continuously adjust the fence. What I did was adjust the fence to cut the slot closes to the flat work surface first. Then I used a small piece of 3/8 inch thick plywood and placed it on the flat work surface for the second cut without the fence. Then finally I used a small piece of 3/ 4 inch plywood on the flat work surface to make the third cut. These fillers allowed me to make all three cuts for the framework of the chair without using the fence.

If you must use the fence, in the interest of accuracy cut all the project pieces first. Set the fence for the first cut and then make all the cuts that will be at that level on every piece of the project. Then adjust the fence for the second cut and make all of those cuts. Finally, adjust the fence for the third cut and make all the third cuts in all the pieces and you are ready to assemble.

Sand Before Assembly: Once you have all your pieces ready for assembly, do all the sanding before you begin. Your project should be ready for the finish once it is assembled. Many projects have inside corners that are difficult to sand properly once assembled. Save yourself all that work by finishing the sanding first.

Choosing The Right Biscuit Size: The choice is simple, always pick the largest biscuit that will fit in the joint that you are creating. This will always give you the maximum amount of glue surface for maximum strength.

In addition to the three basic sizes, 0, 10, and 20, there is a size called FF which stands for Face Frame. This is a smaller size used for attaching face frames to cabinets. There are also some micro size biscuits available for very small jobs but for these you need a smaller, specialized Biscuit Joiner because these biscuits are also thinner. I have not used these smaller sizes as the three regular sizes have always been adequate for my purposes.

Cutting Miter Joints Using Fence at 45 Degrees: In the chapter on Biscuit Joiner methods I show you how to cut the biscuit slots on a mitered corner using the fence set at 90 degrees and at 135 degrees. These are the two methods I believe to be safest and most accurate but you can also make this slot cut by setting the fence at 45 degrees.

For this you would put the fence on the short point side of the board and the face of the Biscuit Joiner against the miter. This method feels less accurate and I recommend one of the two methods previously discussed.

Double Wide Biscuit Slot: For extra strength in extreme situations you can use two biscuits together. This could become necessary on projects that require the extra strength but are constructed of 3/ 4 inch thick material that will not accommodate two separate biscuits.

Using two biscuits requires cutting two slots next to each other. The best way to do this is with a 4 mm (5/32 inch) spacer. You can make a spacer from a piece of scrap plywood or other lumber.

Once you have the spacer, place it under the piece that will be cut and make the first cut. Then remove the spacer and make the second cut and you will have a double biscuit slot. You could also place the spacer under the Biscuit Joiner for the first cut and then remove it for the second cut or vice versa.

Once the double cuts are made, place glue directly on the inside surfaces of the two biscuits, put the glue in the slots, place the biscuits in the slot and then assemble the pieces.

Biscuit Joiner Accessories: I have not made use of the many accessories that are available for biscuit joinery but you may want to look into them. One that I find interesting is the biscuit joiner hinges. These hinges are the shape of biscuits and you use your Biscuit Joiner to cut the mortise for them and then attach them as you would any hinge.

Another item is glueless biscuit clamps. These are half biscuits that are used for gluing boards edge-to-edge. The half biscuit are placed in the biscuit slots without glue and then the boards are placed against each other after the glue is applied to the edges and the biscuits grab each other to keep the boards well aligned.

Another item is metal half biscuits that are tapped tightly into biscuit slots to allow you to create knock down furniture or cabinets. The two biscuits have protrusions that slide into each other to keep the pieces together without glue and allow you to knockdown the pieces later.

A simple accessory made of plastic serves as a simple guide to check the depth for the slot cuts for all three sizes of biscuits. It may be worthwhile to some but certainly not essential to biscuit joinery.

Biscuits Versus Dowels: After visiting many blogs and web sites it's obvious that this is a touchy subject. I believe, and much evidence has shown, that biscuits create stronger joints than dowels. This is simply because biscuits have much more glue surface and that surface is all glued to the long grain of the wood.

Dowels have less glue surface and much of their surface faces the end grain of the wood that does not glue well. In spite of this obvious difference there are running arguments about which of the two provide a stronger joint.

I am not going to participate in that argument. This book is not intended as an attempt to prove that biscuits joints are stronger than dowel joints. It is my opinion based on my years of woodworking experience that they are better, faster, and easier to use but the purpose of this book is to share with you as much information as possible about how you can take advantage of this excellent tool to speed up your work and create quality projects.

Some may wish to spend their time running various tests to prove which is the strongest joint, I prefer to spend my time helping you to built projects faster and better.

Biscuit Joints Versus Mortise and Tenon: This is truly a no brainer. If you have ever built a project using mortise and tenon joinery, as I have, there will be no doubt in your mind that mortise and tenon joints, when done correctly, are considerably stronger than biscuit joints. However, mortise and tenon joinery is truly difficult and time consuming for anyone with limited skills and it's unnecessary for most projects.

Mortise and tenon joinery is an excellent method and if you have the time and inclination I would definitely advise you to try it at least once if for nothing else but the sense of accomplishment.

Other Joinery Methods: There are many other joinery methods including various styles of dovetails, finger joints, dado joints, tongue and groove, just to name a few. They all have their uses and if you decide to use any of them I hope it works for you. For me it isn't a competition, it's simply about getting the projects built. That was always the case when I was operating my woodworking business and it still is now that I build projects only for us.

Notes

Glossary

Alignment: Placing two parts or edges in line with one another.

Allen wrench: A small metal tool consisting of either an L shape or a straight hexagonal rod with a plastic or wood handle. Used to loosen or tighten allen-head screws.

Angle: Normally a line between 0 and 90 degrees.

Apron: The part of a table that normally runs below the tabletop from leg to leg supporting the tabletop and the legs.

Assembly: The work of assembling a project after all the parts have been cut and sanded.

Band Saw: A woodworking power bench saw that uses a metal band blade with teeth that is coupled with two or three wheels. One wheel is powered by a motor and together with the other wheels drives the blade.

Bartley's Gel Varnish: A thick gel like varnish that is applied with a cloth to wood surfaces. It is an excellent product that does not raise the grain on wood.

Bead: A decorative edge design created with a round over router bit set to cut slightly deeper than normal.

Belt Sander: A power sander that uses a circular revolving abrasive belt.

Bench Top: A type of power tool that is used on top of a workbench.

Biscuit: Wood wafers used with biscuit joiners to create a simple and strong joint.

Biscuit Joinery: The kind of joinery that is created by the use of biscuit wafers and biscuit joiners.

Biscuit Slots: The slots cut by a biscuit joiner for the placement of biscuits.

Bosch: A popular brand of routers and sanders made by a German manufacturer.

Brush Marks: The marks created by using a brush on a finish that has begun to dry.

Brushing: The method used to paint or apply clear coats to wood surfaces.

Butt Joints: Simple joints created by simply placing the side of a board against the edge of another board.

Cabinet: A simple box or container with shelves used for storage or display of items.

Cabinet Door: The door for closing a cabinet.

Carbide-tipped: A blade or bit that has carbide tips on the teeth or flutes to maintain sharpness. The carbide is very hard and holds an edge much longer.

Center: The point that is the same distance from two sides.

Centerline: A line marked at the center of a part or project.

Circle: A curved line always an equal distance from a center point.

Clamp: A device for holding wood parts together while glue is drying in the joints.

Clamping: The procedure of holding wood parts together for gluing using clamps.

Clear Coat: A finish applied to wood to beautify and protect the surface without changing its natural look.

Combust Spontaneously: Catching fire suddenly with no apparent cause. Normally happens to rags used to apply oil-based finishes to wood.

Compass: A V shaped device with a sharp point at one end and a pencil at the other used for describing circles or arcs and for taking measurements. Complex Joinery: In comparison to biscuit joinery, other joinery methods such as mortise and tenon joinery.

Compressed Beech: A kind of wood that is placed under great pressure and then cut into oval shapes for use as wafers for biscuit joinery.

Consumer Tools: Lower priced tools made for home use. They are capable of doing much the same work as industrial tools but are not as precise and cannot take the stress often associated with industrial work.

Conversion Kits: Kits that are used to convert grinders and routers into biscuit joiners:

Craftsman: A brand of tools sold at Sears stores.

Crosscut: The procedure of cutting wood across the grain instead of with the grain.

Cut Out: Cutting a section of a certain size and shape from within a project part.

Cutting: The procedure used to turn large panels of wood into the various parts needed for a project.

Dados: A rectangular groove cut into a board to accommodate another wood part.

Decorative: A feature added to a wood project for the sole purpose of decoration.

Decorative Support: A part added to a wood project that serves the dual purpose of decoration and additional strength.

Deft: A quality brand of clear coat that is self-leveling and quick drying.

DeWalt: A manufacturer of quality power tools.

Diagonals: The distance from two extreme opposite corners of a cabinet or other project. Used to determine if the project is square.

Diameter: The length of a line drawn directly through a circle from one side to another going through the center point.

Dimensions: The size of various parts of a project. Usually contains the width, length and thickness.

Dovetails: A complex joinery method involving fan shaped tenons interlocked in a tight joint. Usually used for drawers and used in cabinets to add strength and a decorative touch.

Dowels: A round wood pin that fits into a corresponding hole to align and strength wood joints. Once believed to be a good joinery method but is actually a poor substitute for the biscuit joinery method.

Drawing: A line representation of a project.

Drill: A power tool used to make holes of various sizes in wood.

Drill Press: A bench type power tool used to make precise holes of various sizes in wood.

Drilling: The procedure of using a drill or drill press to make holes in wood.

Drywall Screws: A very sharp specialized screw normally used to fasten sheetrock to a wood or metal studs. These screws are also excellent for the assembly of wood projects.

Dust Bag: A bag attached to a power tool for the purpose of catching the dust that is created while cutting, routing or sanding wood.

Dust Chute: The tube on a power tool that leads to the dust bag.

Edge Joinery: The procedure of jointing the edges of various parts of a wood project.

Eye Protection: Glasses and goggles used to protect the eyes while doing woodworking.

Face Frames: The wood pieces that create the front face of a cabinet or bookcase. Face frames are often decorative but sometimes serve as a base for the cabinet doors.

Fence: The part of a biscuit joiner used to guide the depth and location of a biscuit slot.

Fine Tooth Blade: A blade with small teeth used especially for making smooth cuts in wood. They are especially useful for crosscutting.

Finger Joints: Another joinery method similar to dovetails but without the fan shape. Often used as a decorative feature. They are not as strong as dovetails not as complex.

Finish: The application of a clear or paint coating to a wood project.

Finish Nail: A nail with a small head to facilitate filling of the holes they create in the wood surface.

Finish Sander: A vibrating or orbital sander used for the final sanding of a project before applying the finish.

Flush: Even with or aligned with another surface.

Freehand: Using power tools without some form of guide to make various cuts.

Freud: A brand of power tools manufactured in Spain.

Friction: The rubbing of one surface against another creating heat that can sometimes be damaging.

Furniture: Definitions vary but usually considered as those wood projects not normally considered cabinets. These include chairs, tables and other items for the comfort of people in their home or office.

Glue Bottle Tip: The tip of a bottle used to apply glue to various surfaces and biscuit slots.

Glue Mess: The problem created when too much glue is used to assemble a wood project.

Gluing: The procedure used to glue up project parts.

Gouging: Damage to wood surfaces caused by the improper use of power tools.

Grinders: A power tool used to grind or sand various surfaces and also serves as the power for biscuit joiners.

Half Circle: A curved line that is equal distant from a center point and is only 180 degrees in length.

Hand Sand: The procedure of fine sanding of a project that is done without the use of a power sander.

Handheld: The use of a power tool that is not attached to a bench or table.

High-Speed Steel: A lower quality of blade or bit that requires regular sharpening.

Hobby: Doing woodworking primarily for pleasure.

HVLP Spray Unit: A power spray for project finishes base on a high-volume low-pressure system. There are some excellent, low priced units available.

Industrial Tools: High quality, rugged hand and power tools made especially for professionals.

Instructions: Detailed steps describing specific methods for building projects.

Jigsaw: A power tool with a narrow vertical blade used to cut curves.

Joinery: The procedure of cutting and assembling the joints of a project.

Joinery Methods: The various methods used to join parts of a project.

Kickback: A dangerous incident caused by a piece of wood trapped between a saw blade and a rip fence causing it to be thrown back at the saw operator at high speed.

Kitchen Cabinets: Cabinets built for and installed in the kitchen of a home.

Lacquer: A resinous material used as a surface coating for projects. It has strong vapors and should only be used with a respirator.

Lacquer Thinner: A highly flammable product used to thin and clean lacquer.

Lamello: A brand of biscuit joiner consider industrial grade.

Layout: The arrangement or plan for the building of a project.

Mallet: A short-handled hammer with a large cylindrical or square head made of wood or rubber used to strike objects without damaging them.

Measurements: The dimensions of a certain part or the distances in a project.

MinWax: A brand of stain and clear coat finishes.

Mortise and Tenon: A complex joinery method that creates extreme strong and attractive joints.

Nails: A thin sharp piece of metal hammered into a wood surface as a fastener.

Oil-Based: A finish or other liquid product with an oil base.

Oil-Finishes: A long list of wood finishes with an oil base including tung, linseed and Danish oils.

Oil-Laden Rags: Rags used to apply and wipe off excess oil finishes. It is essential to place such rags in a container filled with water otherwise they can combust spontaneously.

Ooze: The excess glue that is forced out of a joint or biscuit slot when assembled. This excess must be cleaned up completely before applying a finish.

Orbital Sander: A finish sander that works by moving a pad with sandpaper in an rapid orbital pattern over the wood surface.

Orientation: The location and relative position of parts to each other.

Paint Thinner: A liquid used to thin and clean paint and painting tools.

Parts: The pieces of a project prior to being assembled into the whole project.

Pattern: A cardboard or wood piece used to mark other identical pieces for cutting.

Planning: The procedure of designing a project to fit in a certain place or to serve a certain function.

Plate Joiner: Another name sometimes used for biscuit joiner.

Plugs: Small pieces of wood, usually round, used to fill holes containing fasteners of a wood project.

Plywood: A sheet material made of various layers of wood assembled with the grains crossing each other.

Polycrylic: An excellent water-based clear coat that applies easily and makes tools easy to clean.

Polyurethane: A tough, resin-based clear coating for wood projects.

Porter-Cable: A quality brand of power tools. They make an excellent and unique biscuit joiner.

Professional Woodworker: A woodworker who sells his work to customers.

Projects: Any item of furniture or cabinets built of wood.

Push Stick: A simple stick used to push pieces being cut on a saw through the blade to avoid injuries.

Quality Accessories: Addons for various power tools to make them work more effectively.

Quarter Circle: A curved line equal distance from a center point that is only 90 degrees long.

Radius: The distance between the center point of a circle and any point in its circumference.

Random Orbit Sander: A power sander that combines two actions. One action is circular and removes the most material. The second action is orbital and removes the marks created by the circular motion.

Recoat: The application of another coat of finish to a project.

Rectangular: A shape containing four right angles with two sides that are longer than the other two sides.

Reinforced Butt Joints: A butt joint that is reinforced by biscuits or some other form of joinery.

Respirator: A device worn over the mouth and nose to protect the respiratory system from dangerous vapors.

Rip: Cutting wood with the grain.

Round Over Bit: A router bit that creates a quarter round cut of the edges of wood.

Rout: The cutting done by a router bit on a wood surface or edge.

Router: A power tool that is used to cut various shapes in wood, including decorative edges, dados, rabbets, etc.

Router Kits: Used to convert routers for use as a biscuit joiner.

Router Table: Used to hold a router in a permanent position while moving the piece to be routed past the router bit. This is much safer when working with small wood parts.

Rubbing: A method for applying and removing excess finishing materials.

Ryobi: A Japanese manufacturer of quality consumer power tools.

Safety Guidelines: Rules for using power tools safely.

Sanding: The procedure of smoothing wood surfaces in preparation for a finish.

Sanding Drum: A small attachment for a drill that facilitates the sanding on inside round surfaces that cannot be reached with standard sanding tools.

Sandpaper: Paper coated on one side with abrasive materials for smoothing wood surfaces.

Satin: A slightly dull finish used on some projects.

Screw Holes: Holes drilled to facilitate driving screws into wood without causing cracking.

Screws: A metal pin with incised threads and a slotted or Phillips head to be driven into a wood surface by a screwdriver.

Scroll Saw: A power saw with a narrow, thin blade used to cut very irregular shapes.

Self-Tapping: Screw with a special point that creates a hole for itself as it is driven. They preclude the need for pre-drilling holes.

Self-Leveling: A finish that levels out the brush marks before it dries on a wood surface.

Semi-Gloss: A finish with a low sheen often preferred over high gloss for projects.

Shelf Edges: The edges of the wood shelves in a project. The edges can be covered with veneer or with a decorative wood edge.

Shelves: Part of a cabinet or bookcase used to hold and store objects or books.

Simplified Methods: Methods developed to make woodworking easier and faster.

Simplified Woodworking: A set of methods designed to make woodworking faster and more profitable.

Skil: A power tool manufacturer that makes both consumer and industrial tools.

Special Glue Bottles: Bottles used to apply glue to biscuit joints without creating ooze.

Square: Indicating a right angle that is exactly 90 degrees.

Stain: A colored penetrating liquid, dye or tint used to change the color of wood before applying a clear coat.

Straight Edge: A piece of wood or metal used as a guide to make a line or to align two or more parts.

Streaks: Unattractive stain marks in a project finish left because of improper or inadequate wiping of an applied stain.

Supports: Wood parts assembled in a project for the purpose of strengthening it.

Table Saw: A bench power tools that facilitates guided cuts to crosscut and rip wood.

Tack Cloth: A varnish soaked cloth used to remove dust from a project before applying a finish.

Taper Jig: A guide that is made or purchased to facilitate the safe cutting of various angles on a table saw.

Test Cut: A cut made in a scrap piece of wood to make certain that a specific power tool is properly set up before cutting the actual work piece.

Toe Board: The board at the base of a project.

Traditional: Methods that have been used for many years.

Transfer: Running a mark from one location on a specific part to another.

Trim Screws: A special kind of drywall screws that have a small head like a finish nail. This facilitates the use of wood filler to cover the screw heads.

Unclamp: Removing the clamps on a project after the glue dries.

V Mark: A mark used on the back of a glued up table surface to make certain that the pieces are assembled in the planned order.

Varnish: A coating containing a solvent and binder used to apply a glossy and transparent finish to wood projects.

Virutex: A quality brand of biscuit joiner made by a Spanish manufacturer of power and hand tools.

Wafer: The compressed beech product used in biscuit slots as part of the biscuit joinery method. They are also known as biscuits.

Water-Based: Finishes that have a water base and can be cleaned using only water.

White Pine: An attractive and relatively inexpensive wood that can be used for wood projects.

Wipe Off: The procedure used to remove excess stain and unattractive streaks.

Wood Edging: Also known as veneer edging, it is very thin wood usually applied to the edges of plywood using hot melt glue.

Wood Filler: A soft, creamy product used to fill nail or screw holes. It is sometimes purchased as a powder that can be mixed with water.

Woodworkers Vise: A bench vise with wood jaws that facilitates clamping wood parts without pressure damage.

Woodworking Business: The business of making and selling wood projects of various kinds on speculation or as commissions to customers for profit.

Workbench: A bench designed especially for woodworking with vises and other attachments that facilitate building projects.

Worktable: Any table or bench used to cut and assemble wood projects.

Notes

DISCLAIMER

Everything described in this book is based on my personal experience. I owned and operated a full-time woodworking business for over thirty years, first in Tampa, Florida and then in Austin, Texas. During most of those years I used Biscuit Joiners to build hundreds of projects for many customers and for myself and learned many ways to take full advantage of the capabilities of the Biscuit Joiner as a wood joinery tool. This book attempts to convey as much of that knowledge as possible to others so they can experience the same benefits. Nevertheless, no guarantees are expressed or implied regarding your own results using the information in this book.

This book was written based entirely on first-hand experience so that every method described and pictured was actually performed many times on many projects. I personally designed, built, and photographed every project shown in this book so I know these methods work.

I believe anyone with some woodworking skills can use a Biscuit Joiner to perform the work described especially if they practice with the simple project plans included in this book. Toward that end I have included detailed instructions, drawings, and photographs to clarify the methods. Nevertheless, it's impossible to know the skill level and capabilities of readers so I can't guarantee you will be able to successfully perform the tasks described herein.

In addition to the Biscuit Joiner, woodworking involves the use of an extensive collection of tools capable of inflicting serious injuries. I have made every effort to accurately describe my experiences with the Biscuit Joiner in detail, including safety considerations with it and other power tools, but I cannot be held liable for any damages or injuries resulting from the use of this information even if the user informs me prior to or after these damages or injuries occur.

This book includes the names of and information about several brand name products. Many of these are products I have personally used as indicated in the book and others have been highly recommended to me. I own no interest in any of the manufacturers or distributors of these products nor have I received any payment for listing them in this book. They are listed only as part of my experience and for informational purposes.

The user of this information agrees he or she is solely responsible for the consequences of using the Biscuit Joiner or any other tools or products described in this book. The information contained and distributed in this book is not intended as nor should it be considered professional, business, or legal advice.

For any questions please contact bill@positive-imaging.com

A. William (Bill) Benitez,
BIOGRAPHICAL INFORMATION

Bill Benitez was born into construction. From age twelve he spent his summers and weekends working with his father, a general contractor, building homes and buildings. At age nineteen he contracted and built his first house for a customer and then built his own home at age twenty. He has over 30 years experience operating one-person businesses.

For more than 12 years Bill Benitez worked for local government in Tampa, Florida running federally-assisted housing programs. He started as an inspector and was Director of Community Improvement when he resigned to do writing and consulting. His experience in housing rehabilitation is extensive and in 1977 he was invited to testify before the United States Congress on housing issues.

For six years, Bill owned and operated Rehab Notes Library, that published a monthly newsletter (Rehab Notes) with subscribers in all 50 states, Canada and England. He provided consulting and public speaking services to agencies and organizations in cities across the country. He was instrumental in the development of several community housing programs involving partnerships between local banks and government agencies. During this period he also wrote several guidebooks on the subject including one that was published by the National Association of Housing and Redevelopment Officials. These books include:

1. **Housing Rehabilitation: A Guidebook for Municipal Programs**, Published by: The National Association of Housing and Redevelopment Officials 1976

2. **So You Want To Do Rehab: A Local Official's Guide To Housing Rehabilitation**, Published by: Florida Department of Community Affairs 1977
3. **How To Involve Contractors in Housing Rehabilitation**, Published by: Rehab Notes Library 1978
4. **The Best of Rehab Notes 1977**, Published by: Rehab Notes Library 1977
5. **Regulations and Guidelines: A Guide form for A Housing Rehabilitation Financing Handbook**, Published by: Rehab Notes Library 1978
6. **How To Develop and Operate A Successful Housing Rehabilitation Program**, Published by: Rehab Notes Library 1978
7. **A Contractor's Guide To Federally Assisted Housing Rehabilitation**, Published by: Rehab Notes Library 1979
8. **Financing Housing Rehabilitation: A Local Official's Guide To Leveraging**, Published by: Rehab Notes Library 1979
9. **A Private Lender's Guide To Involvement In Federally Assisted Housing Rehabilitation**, Published by: Rehab Notes Library 1980
10. **The Rehabilitation Specialist Guidebook**, Published by: Rehab Notes Library 1980

During this same period he did consulting jobs for many agencies and companies including:

- The Florida Department of Community Affairs
- University Research Corporation, Washington, DC
- Cincinnati Rehabilitation Loan Corporation
- Ohio Conference of Community Development
- Planned Management Corporation, Tampa, Florida
- R. A. Smith and Associates, Tampa, Florida
- City of Kansas City, Missouri
- Louisville Urban Renewal Agency
- City of Ocala, Florida
- Kentucky Housing and Community Development Association
- National Association of Housing and Redevelopment Officials, Washington, DC
- City of Wichita, Kansas
- Miami Valley Regional Planning Commission, Ohio
- Summit County Planning Department, Akron, Ohio

- Rehabilitation Loan Corporation, Kansas City, Missouri
- South Central Illinois Regional Planning Commission
- League of Women Voters, Springfield Ohio
- City of Hopkinsville, Kentucky
- City of Tallahassee, Florida.

After 1980 when the housing assistance programs were cut back, Bill started a woodworking business based on his construction experience. He also began writing about his experiences and published a book and project newsletters on woodworking.

During this time he wrote **SIMPLIFIED WOODWORKING I: A Business Guide For Woodworkers**. He also wrote and published the monthly project newsletter **SIMPLIFIED WOODWORKING** for two years and conducted power tool demonstrations for the Skil Power Tool Company. Sometime later he encapsulated his self-employment experience in **THE SELF EMPLOYMENT SURVIVAL MANUAL: How to Start and Operate a One-Person Business Successfully**. Both of these books are now out of print.

In 1996 he began studying computers and is now a certified computer expert with A+ and MCSE certifications. Now he uses his computer skills together with his writing and publishing experience to operate Positive Imaging, LLC a publishing company that publishes books and ebooks he writes and also for other authors. You can check out all the books he has written and published on his web site at http://positive-imaging.com .

Bill Benitez lived in Tampa, Florida until 1986 when he moved to Austin, Texas. He now lives in Austin with his wife Barbara Frances.

Notes

OTHER PUBLICATIONS FROM POSITIVE IMAGING, LLC

Paperback

Woodworking Business:
Start Quickly And Operate Successfully
by A. William Benitez
http://woodworkingbusinessbook.com

The Handyman's Guide To Profit
Using Your Skills To Make Money In Any Economy
by A. William Benitez
http://handyman-business-guide.com

Self Publishing:
How To Publish Your Print Book or eBook
Step by Step
by A. William Benitez
http://selfpublishingworkbook.com

Lottie's Adventure:
Facing The Monster
by Barbara Frances
http://lottiesadventure.com

Peace And Healing For The World Using Altars
Lucretia Jones and Gaila Slaughter
http://peaceandhealingfortheworld.com

The End Of All Worries:
We Are All One
by Irie Glajar
http://the-end-of-all-worries.com

Teach For Life
Essays On Modern Education For Teachers, Students, and Parents
by Irie Glajar
http://teachforlife.positive-imaging.com

Escape To Freedom
Chronicles Of A Life On Two Continents
My Escape From Communist Romania
An Autobiography
By Irie Glajar
http://escapetofreedom.positive-imaging.com

Deep Photographs
The Education of a Sociologist
by David Weiner
https://www.createspace.com/3723277

Digital Books (ebooks)

Lottie's Adventure:
Facing The Monster
by Barbara Frances
https://www.smashwords.com/books/view/25753

The Handyman's Guide To Profit
Using Your Skills To Make Money In Any Economy
by A. William Benitez
https://www.smashwords.com/books/view/28293

Relationship: Notes on Love, Mutual Respect, Boundaries, Marriage, and Divorce
by A. William Benitez
https://www.smashwords.com/books/view/26219

Teach For Life
Essays On Modern Education For Teachers, Students, and Parents
by Irie Glajar
https://www.smashwords.com/books/view/42694

Woodworking Business:
Start Quickly And Operate Successfully

Woodworking skills are important to the success of a woodworking business but many other business skills are also required. After years in construction I started my woodworking business but it still took time to hone the skills needed to make the business profitable. After almost thirty years operating a woodworking business I share those proven successful techniques in my book "Woodworking Business: Start Quickly And Operate Successfully."

If you are already a competent woodworker wanting to start a woodworking business, or already in the woodworking business but would like to increase your profit and simplify your work, "Woodworking Business: Start Quickly And Operate Successfully" is for you.

Get complete information now at: http://woodworking-business.com

Also check out my woodworking web sites and blogs at:

http://woodworkdoctor.com

http://www.woodworking-biz-solutions.com

http://woodworking-business.com/woodworkbiz

Questions or comments? Please contact me at:
bill@positive-imaging.com

Notes

www.ingramcontent.com/pod-product-compliance
Lightning Source LLC
LaVergne TN
LVHW081318110826
845149LV00006B/1541

* 9 7 8 0 9 8 5 6 8 7 6 2 5 *